W9-BBI-377

PRAYERS OF THE WOMEN MYSTICS

Prayers of
the Women Mystics

✠ ✠ ✠

Ronda De Sola Chervin

Servant Publications
Ann Arbor, Michigan

Copyright © 1992 Ronda De Sola Chervin
All rights reserved.

See bibliography for a list of resources used by the author.

Published by Servant Publications
P.O. Box 8617
Ann Arbor, Michigan 48107

Cover design by Micah Piccirilli

93 94 95 96 10 9 8 7 6 5 4 3 2

Printed in the United States of America

ISBN 0-89283-750-0

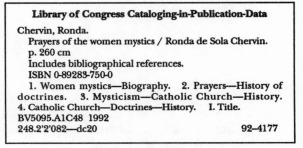

Library of Congress Cataloging-in-Publication-Data

Chervin, Ronda.
  Prayers of the women mystics / Ronda de Sola Chervin.
    p. 260 cm
  Includes bibliographical references.
  ISBN 0-89283-750-0
    1. Women mystics—Biography. 2. Prayers—History of
doctrines. 3. Mysticism—Catholic Church—History.
4. Catholic Church—Doctrines—History. I. Title.
BV5095.A1C48 1992
248.2'2'082—dc20   92–4177

Contents

Introduction

A WOMAN CLAIMS TO HAVE HEARD an audible voice in prayer. Another woman claims to have experienced a deep, indescribable union with God while in prayer. What are we to make of apparent mystical experiences like these?

Are these the sorts of images that tend to surface when you think of the word "mysticism"? Does the word carry positive or negative connotations? For some, the word is positive, describing the ecstatic happiness that often marks the experience of one who is intimate with God, especially in prayer. For others, the word is negative and even frightening, conjuring up the image of a gullible and imbalanced person who has an overly excitable imagination. For still others, the word is a jumble of negative and positive associations, depending upon the context and the particular mystic cited. Some think that those with a more intuitive, imaginative, and artistic bent tend to be more open to mysticism.

Speaking for myself, I first heard of Catholic

mysticism as a new convert. Coming from an atheistic background with Jewish roots, the word conjured up for me a mixture of skepticism and fascination. The Catholic faith itself seemed to be full of mystical elements. In our creed, we professed to believe in a God who was the Light of Lights. In the church, we believed that we were united to each other as members of the mystical body of Christ. Yet most Catholics I met seemed to have their feet solidly planted on the ground. Their hope of ecstatic happiness or mystical oneness with God seemed centered on dreams of glory in heaven. There seemed to be a gap between doctrine and teaching on the one hand and personal knowledge and experience on the other.

Happily, at this juncture I met another Jewish convert, a lay contemplative named Charles Rich. This fiery soul was devoted to introducing Catholics to the writings of the Western mystics. Reading Teresa of Avila, John of the Cross, Francis de Sales, and many others was exciting and tantalizing. Yet it also produced holy envy. Why did some of God's children seem to experience such spectacular graces, while others remained in what seemed the lowlands of rote prayer?

Even though I myself had little experience of supernatural graces, I found the words of the mystics invigorating. They extended my horizons and gave me a small but real foretaste of God's passionate love for his creatures.

I was especially drawn to the autobiography of St. Teresa of Avila. A religious celibate, she nevertheless experienced the problem of infatuation with men. Remarkably, this longstanding difficulty and distraction was resolved through her experience of seeing the radiant face and form of Christ so vividly that never again was she hindered by infatuation with a mere earthly man.

Yet it was only many years after my first reading of the great mystics that I began to experience something mystical myself. It seemed to start when I was interceding to the Virgin Mary and was suddenly overwhelmed by a sense of deep, inner peace. This peace seemed to permeate every cell of my being, and I was usually a very restless and nervous person at that time. It settled around me like a sort of cloud, especially when I prayed. This experience lasted almost a year, during which time my mind was illuminated by a much more vivid understanding of divine truth than ever before. Simultaneously, I would be awakened at night by a fiery desire for union with God that would fill me with awe, wonder, and delight.

After such personal experiences, I read the mystics with renewed interest and understanding. Their writings echoed the melodies that the Holy Spirit seemed to be singing within my own heart. I also found resonances of the pain that inevitably accompanies such an expansion of consciousness. I came to understand how contemplative bliss is always interwoven with the trials that purify the Christian soul of dross—impurities which become even more visible in the great light of God's holiness.

In giving workshops and retreats on spirituality and writing about women's issues, I have come to an even deeper appreciation of women saints and holy women mystics as our foremothers, revelatory of what I regard as genuine in feminine spirituality.

A WORD ABOUT MYSTICISM AND MY SELECTIONS

The women I have chosen to write about are all mystics. But why do we speak of some religious figures as mystics and describe others in different terms?

On the one hand, there are many believers in God who have a strong personal faith and much holiness of life, exhibited by their love of God and neighbor. But they do not experience much of a felt sense of God drawing them into a supernatural union with himself. The important thing is that such persons continue to follow God as he leads and reveals himself. After all, mystical experience is not, in and of itself, necessarily a sign of holiness.

On the other hand, there are believers of God who not only exhibit personal faith and holiness of life, but feel consciously drawn into a closer supernatural union with God. Such a union may manifest itself in a variety of ways, ranging from a quiet but profound sense of God's presence to hearing an audible voice in prayer, or even seeing a vision while in prayer. Such believers are properly called mystics when experiences like these begin to typify their spiritual life.

However, it is important to stress that the fruit of true mystical prayer is heroic virtue and not the ecstatic experiences themselves. In fact, some who experience extraordinary mystical states are deluded and may be under the control of evil spiritual forces. This becomes especially clear when their lives produce bad fruit. Mystical experience, if authentic and God-centered, is fundamentally a grace from God which will draw us closer to him and our brothers and sisters. If we respond to it properly, it will produce good fruit in our lives.

That said, we should strive for balance when assessing our attitude toward authentic mystical experience and the prayer life it engenders. While we should never seek such experience as a tonic for boredom in routine prayer, we should always remain open to whatever grace God might give for our sanctification and purification of heart. We know that unless his love fills us to overflowing, we will never be able to love him and our neighbor to the degree we so ardently wish. Sanctity includes the self-emptying and union with God that has come to many through mystical graces. We should never refuse such a precious gift of God.

A word about the different *types* of prayer selected for *Prayers of the Women Mystics.* The plaintive cry that issues most often from the pens of the mystics is the impossibility of conveying the ineffable beauty of the realities given to them in visions or invisible intuitions. I am so thankful that they tried nonetheless.

Most often the prayer of a mystic is in the form of either silent infusions of love or locutions. Silent infusions of love occur when warm feelings suddenly flood the soul and direct it toward God. Locutions are words from God. They are not necessarily heard with the human ear, but they are understood by the heart.

Consequently, the prayers of the mystics are usually not their own words but the words of God, written down after the reception of such graces. However, some mystics take pleasure in writing prayers, poems, or songs in their own voice. Inevitably, these utterances exude the same fragrance of their more wordless experiences.

In view of the variety of forms offered in books of the mystics, I have used my own discernment in selecting some prayers of a more conventional form along with other passages dictated to the mystic by Persons of the Blessed Trinity, angels, or the Virgin Mary. Sometimes I have simply excerpted from their lovely, lyrical poetry.

Some saints, perhaps more widely known than those I have chosen to include, are better described under other categories then mysticism. In general, among the many possibilities of women mystics, I have chosen those whose spirituality is most formed by the mystical graces they received. For example, it would be impossible to describe the journey of a St. Catherine of Siena without reference to the locutions she received from God. By comparison, someone like St. Thérèse of Lisieux is more extraordinary in her surrender to a life of pure faith than in her response to specific mystical graces. Others, such as Blessed Edith Stein, are more of interest for the way God's providence mingled their particular gifts with dramatic circumstances.

If you are using *Prayers of the Women Mystics* for meditation, I suggest that you first read aloud the selections and then peruse them again slowly and silently. As you do, allow these rapturous outpourings of love to lead you into your own prayer. You may want to keep a journal in which to record your own reflections and graces. After all, you are as precious in God's sight as any famous contemplative. Whenever I would get carried away by a slavish desire to imitate a particular mystic, one of my mentors, Fr. Rockwell Shaules, S.J., used to remark: "God already has St. Catherine of Siena. Now he wants St. Ronda."

Remember that you need not have received mystical experiences yourself to be inspired by these women mystics. All of us should desire an intimate union with God, whether it is accompanied by mystical graces or not. Hence, we can all be inspired by these women who were first and foremost frail human beings who desired to be holy as God is holy. Our horizons can be expanded as we observe the various ways God worked in the lives of these women as they responded to his graces.

A word of caution. All spiritual directors warn us that it is fruitless and even counter-productive to force oneself to meditate on materials that are personally uninviting. For whatever reason, if you have an "allergic" reaction to any one of the mystics in this book, I encourage you to simply skip around until you find one who is your true soul-sister.

I am thankful for this opportunity to share some of my favorite holy sisters with you. My hope and prayer is that you will be enkindled by their writings to seek your own rendezvous with God each day and to be open as he leads you deeper into his burning love. Let us join hands across these pages and pray that the Holy Spirit may bring us safely from time to eternity on the wings of prayer. Amen! Alleluia!

1

Saint Hildegard of Bingen
(1098–1179)

Holy ones of old! You foretold deliverance for the souls of exiles slumped in the dead lands. Like wheels you spun round in wonder as you spoke of the mysterious mountain at the brink of heaven that stills many waters, sailing over the waves. And a shining lamp burned in the midst of you!... And you, fire-breathing voice, chewing the cud of the word, racing to the touchstone that topples hell: rejoice in your captain. Rejoice in whom many though they called on him ardently saw not upon earth. Rejoice in your captain.

Antiphon for Patriarchs and Prophets by St. Hildegard[1]

✠ ✠ ✠

HILDEGARD WAS the last of ten children born into a noble and wealthy family.[2] At the age of eight, as was not uncommon in those days, she was entrusted to the care of a relative, a nun named Blessed Jutta, the recluse. Jutta taught the girl to read the Bible in Latin and to chant the Office.

When other women later joined Jutta in the formation of a Benedictine convent, Hildegard followed. Her early life in the monastery was outwardly uneventful but full of interior graces. She saw many things of a spiritual nature that no one else could see and was especially known for her prophecies about future events.

When Blessed Jutta died, Hildegard became the prioress of the monastery. Though weak of health, this saintly woman possessed an unusually gifted mind and unquenchable energy. Hildegard began writing at the age of forty-three. Her works cover a wide range of styles and topics, including poetry, drama, history, politics, herbal medicine, and the liturgical songs compiled in the *Symphonia*. One of her books in the area of medicine, which included the diagnosis of psychological disorders, is now being mined as a source for homeopathic cures. Hildegard was also widely sought after as a counselor.

At the age of sixty this holy nun undertook preaching tours aimed at church reform. Because the times were so evil and filled with many lukewarm priests, Hildegard was strengthened in the idea that she was called to fill the gap by teaching, preaching, and prophesying. She received the approval of ecclesiastical authority for this apostolate.

For all these acts, St. Hildegard was deemed an unusually courageous woman. Her assertive challenges to weak churchmen may lead some admirers of our times to think of this bold nun as a feminist figure. That is certainly true if this means being a strong woman in leadership, but not if such a description means being a revisionist. St. Hildegard's writings abound in expressions of obedience to Catholic doctrine and disgust with heresy. She also explicitly affirmed the non-admission of women to the priesthood.[3]

St. Hildegard is best known for her mystical writings of which the *Scivias* is the most famous— otherwise known as *Scito vias Domini* or *Know the Ways of the Lord.* When she was forty-three years old, a fiery light inflamed her whole mind and heart resulting in infused wisdom about Scripture. The opening passages in *Scivias* give an idea of the forcefulness of her mission:

> And behold! In the forty-third year of my earthly course, as I was gazing with great fear and trembling attention at a heavenly vision, I saw a great splendor in which resounded a voice from Heaven, saying to me, "O fragile human, ashes of ashes, and filth of filth! Say and write what you see and hear. But since you are timid in speaking, and simple in expounding, and untaught in writing, speak and write these things not by a human mouth, and not by the understanding of human invention, and not by the requirements of human composition, but as you see and hear them on high in the heavenly places

in the wonders of God."[4]

"Cry out and speak of the origin of pure salvation until those people are instructed, who, though they see the inmost contents of the Scriptures, do not wish to tell them or preach them, because they are lukewarm and sluggish in serving God's justice. Unlock for them the enclosure of mysteries that they, timid as they are, conceal in a hidden and fruitless field. Burst forth into a fountain of abundance and overflow with mystical knowledge, until they who now think you contemptible because of Eve's transgression are stirred up by the flood of your irrigation."[5]

St. Hildegard's charisms were affirmed by no less a churchman than St. Bernard of Clairvaux and finally endorsed by Pope Eugenius III. Some of these visions were prophetic, like the one ordering her to build her own monastery at Rupertsberg. Hildegard's letters to popes, emperors, bishops, abbots, and kings concerned revelations about disasters that would come unless some improvement was made in the behavior of the lax clergy. After she died in 1179, many miracles were attributed to her intercession.

St. Hildegard's spirituality reflects not so much a bride-soul as a visionary.[6] A famous passage reveals the essence of her visionary gift:

From my infancy until now, in the seventieth year of my age, my soul has always beheld this Light; and in it my soul soars to the summit of the firmament and into a different air.... The brightness which I see is not limited by space and is more brilliant than the radiance around the Sun.... Sometimes when I see it, all sadness and pain is lifted from me, and I seem a simple girl again, and an old woman no more.[7]

Hildegard's spirituality is Benedictine and therefore not predominantly ascetical. Her key images focus on the bright light of divine truth rather than ecstatic feelings. Instead of her own subjective responses, Hildegard is more concerned with the motives for praise and with the supernatural truths to be transmitted through her to the church. Most of her prayer was visionary. The ones written in her own voice are scripturally and liturgically based.

I have selected for meditation the praise-prayers of St. Hildegard found in the *Symphonia*, the collection of her liturgical songs, primarily because I find them to be the most beautiful of her writings. In a media-dominated world strewn with dull or shocking prose, our souls thirst for the spirit of poetry.

We can seek refreshment in our prayer from the moving lyricism of Scripture and the writings of saints like Hildegard. We can also be open to the Holy Spirit gracing us with poetic expression. Keeping a spiritual journal is one way to save the fruits of our intimate conversations with the Lord of all beauty.

IN PRAISE OF GOD

Note how Hildegard weaves homey, sensory imagery into her awe at the marvelous drama of salvation.

Strength of the everlasting!
In your heart you invented
order.

Then you spoke the word and
all that you ordered was,
just as you wished.
And your word put on vestments
woven of flesh
cut from a woman
born of Adam
to bleach the agony out of his clothes.

The Saviour is grand and kind!
from the breath of God he took flesh
unfettered
(for sin was not in it)
to set everything free
and bleach the agony out of his clothes.

Glorify the Father,
The Spirit and the Son.

He bleached the agony out of his clothes.[8]

O handiwork of God,
O human form divine!
In great holiness
you were fashioned,
for the Holy One pierced the heavens
in great humility
and the splendor of God shone forth
in the slime of the earth:
the angels that minister on high
see heaven clothed in humanity.[9]

Praise to you
Spirit of fire!
to you who sound the timbrel
and the lyre.

Your music sets our minds
ablaze! The strength of our souls
awaits your coming
in the tent of meeting.

There the mounting will
gives the soul its savor
and desire is its lantern.

Insight invokes you in a cry
full of sweetness, while reason
builds you temples as she labors
at her golden crafts.

But sword
in hand you stand poised

to prune shoots of the poisoned
apple—
scions of the darkest
murder—

when mist overshadows the will.
Adrift in desires the soul is spinning
everywhere. But the mind
is a bond
to bind will and desire.

When the heart yearns to look
the Evil One in the eye,
to stare down the jaws of
iniquity, swiftly
you burn it in consuming
fire. Such is your wish.

And when reason doing ill
falls from her place, you
restrain and constrain her as you will
in the flow of experience until
she obeys you.

And when the Evil One brandishes
his sword against you,
you break it in his own
heart. For so you did
to the first lost angel,
tumbling the tower of his
arrogance to hell.

And there you built a second
tower—traitors and sinners
its stones. In repentance
they confessed all their crafts.

So all beings that live by you
praise your outpouring
like a priceless salve upon [festering]
sores, upon fractured
limbs. You convert them
into priceless gems!

Now gather us all to yourself
and in your mercy guide us
into the paths of justice.[10]

Spirited light! on the edge
of the Presence your yearning
burns in the secret darkness, O angels, insatiably
into God's gaze.

Perversity
could not touch your beauty;
you are essential joy.
But your lost companion,
angel of the crooked
wings—he sought the summit,
shot down the depths of God
and plummeted past Adam—
that a mud-bound spirit might soar.[11]

PRAYERS TO MARY

*Note how these prayers are full of feminine sweetness
without the least sentimentality.*

Radiant
mother of sacred healing!
you poured salve on the sobbing
wounds that Eve sculpted
to torment our souls.
For your salve is your son and you
wrecked death forever,
sculpturing life.

Pray for us to your child,
Mary, star of the sea.

O life-giving source and gladdening
sign and sweetness of all
delights that flow unfailing!

Pray for us to your child,
Mary, star of the sea.

Glorify the Father,
the Spirit and the Son.

Pray for us to your child,
Mary, star of the sea.[12]

A royal scepter and a crown
of purple, a fortress
strong as mail! O fortress

of maidenhood, scepter
all verdant:

The way you bloomed would have startled
the grandsire of us all,
for the life father Adam
stripped from his sons (praise
to you!) slid from your loins.

You never sprang from the dew,
my blossom, nor from the rain—
that was no wind that swept
over you—for God's
radiance opened you
on a regal bough. On the morn
of the universe he saw you
blossoming, and he made you
a golden matrix, O maid
beyond praise, for his word.

Strong rib of Adam! Out of you
God sculpted woman: the mirror
of all his charms, the caress
of his whole creation. So voices
chime in heaven and the whole
earth marvels at Mary,
beloved beyond measure.

Cry, cry aloud! A serpent
hissed and a sea of grief
seeped through his forked

words into woman. The mother
of us all miscarried.
With ignorant hands she
plucked at her womb and bore
woe without bounds.

But the sunrise from your thighs
burnt the whole of her guilt away.
More than all that Eve lost
is the blessing you won.

Mary, savior,
mother of light:
may the limbs of your son be the chords of the
    song
that angels chant above.[13]

Priceless integrity!
Her virgin gate
opened to none. But the Holy One
flooded her with warmth
until a flower sprang in her womb
and the Son of God came forth
from her secret chamber like the dawn.

Sweet as the buds of spring, her
son opened paradise
from the cloister of her womb.
And the Son of God came forth
from her secret chamber like the dawn.[14]

SUPPLICATION FOR THE CHURCH

How modern are some of St. Hildegard's plaintive pleas for mercy and renewal for the church—made up always of frail men and women, yet beloved still of the Christ who formed her.

Ecclesia, mourn!
Virgin, lament!
That savage
wolf—shame
on that snake!—
has snatched your sons.
Cursed be his cunning!
But the savior
raises his
standard,
he ransoms
all with his blood—
he makes you his bride![15]

Let Mother Ecclesia
sing for joy!
Her children are found,
she gathers them home
to celestial harmony.
But you, vile serpent,
lie low! For those
your jealousy held in its maw
now shine in the blood of Christ.

Praise to our King,
praise to the Highest!
Alleluia.[16]

O glistening starlight,
O royal bride-elect,
resplendent, O sparkling
gem: you are robed
like a noble lady
without spot or wrinkle.
Companion of angels,
fellow citizen with saints—
flee, flee the ancient
destroyer's cave and come—
come into the palace of the King.[17]

2

Blessed Angela of Foligno
(1248–1309)

I was uplifted in spirit, and the Blessed Virgin appeared unto me in a vision and said: "Oh my daughter, sweet unto my Son and unto me, My Son is now come unto thee and thou hast received His blessing.... Forasmuch as thou hast received the blessing of my Son, it is meet that I should come unto thee and give thee mine likewise.... Be thou blessed of my Son and of me, and strive thou with all diligence and earnestness to love Him to the utmost of thy power; for thou art greatly beloved and shalt attain unto that which is infinite."[1]

✠ ✠ ✠

ONE OF THE MOST DRAMATIC of women mystics was Blessed Angela. Born in a town twenty miles from Assisi about thirty years after the death of St. Francis, she married young and had seven children. Angela describes herself in her famous autobiographical treatise, *The Book of Divine Con-*

solation, as a most sinful woman, presumably an adulteress.

In her late thirties, Angela made a pilgrimage to Assisi. The grace of a sudden and tremendous conversion led her to become a Third Order Franciscan. Even though her circumstances seemed contradictory, Angela was aflame with yearning to change her life. Here is a typical description of her early difficulties:

There was given unto me the desire to seek out and know the way of the Cross, that I might stand at its foot and find refuge there where all sinners find refuge. Unto which end I was enlightened and instructed after this manner: that if I did desire to find the way and come unto the Cross, I must first pardon all those who had offended me, and must then put away from me all earthly things, not only out of mine affections but likewise in very deed, and all men and women, friends and kindred and every other thing, but more especially my possessions must I put away, and even mine own self. And I must give my heart unto Christ... electing to walk upon the thorny path, which is the path of tribulation. So then I did begin to put aside the best clothing and garments which I had and the most delicate food.... But as yet it was a shameful and a hard thing for me to do, seeing that I did not feel much love for God and was living with mine husband. Wherefore was it a bitter thing for me when any offence was said or done unto me, but I did bear it as patiently as I was able. In that time and by God's will there died my mother, who was a great hindrance unto me in following the way of God; my husband died likewise, and in a short time there also died all my children.[2]

After these deaths—probably caused by plague—Angela decided to cloister herself from the world near the church of the Franciscan Friars of Foligno. She longed for poverty and penance as a way to break free from bondage to the vanities so commonly associated with the social life of that time.

After this decision, Blessed Angela—like many other mystics—soon found herself on a roller-coaster of glorious joys and unbearable interior sufferings. She describes some of her first consolations in this manner:

> I so greatly delighted in prayer that I did forget to eat. Wherefore did I wish that there were no need for eating, in order that I might be ever at prayer.... There was such a great fire of love in mine heart that I did never weary of being upon my knees, or of doing other penance. After this I was filled with a yet greater fire and fervour of Divine love, in such a degree that if I did hear any man speaking of God I did cry aloud, and even had there been one with an axe ready to kill me I could not have refrained.[3]

Soon other followers began to gather around Angela in the cell-like house where she dwelled with one woman companion. Together this group engaged in prayer, penance, and care of the sick.

For a period of almost two years, Blessed Angela was afflicted with demonic temptations. She reports that some of these enticing ideas concerned sins she had never even imagined in the evil days of her youth: "Not only did I remember those vices which assailed me in times past, but many others which I did never before know entered into my body and did inflame me and cause me the utmost suffering."[4]

In her vivid description of that time of temptation, the widowed contemplative wrote that she felt like "one who is hanged by the neck, his hands tied behind his back and his eyes bound, and who is left hanging by rope upon the gallows; and although he hath no help or remedy or support, he doth nevertheless continue to live in that torment and cannot die."[5] The saint eventually discerned that God had given her these torments to overcome the pride that would otherwise have attended her magnificent special gifts in mystical prayer.

Blessed Angela's account of her life in union with God was dictated to her confessor and contained in *The Book of Divine Consolation*. Originally in Latin, it was translated back into Angela's Italian in 1510 and popularly distributed. She soon became one of the most beloved women mystical writers of Europe.

In his introduction to this book, Algar Thorold writes that Blessed Angela's life and writings are typical of Franciscan spirituality in their immediate unity of thought and action and their candid and passionate narrative style.[6] Her extremely emotional responses to infused grace are contrasted with the detached mood of Eastern mysticism. Angela is deemed to be a prime example of the way contemplation of the figure of Christ is able to act like a "lens... [which can] focus the rays of Divinity and unite them in a shaft of light on which [one] can gaze without faltering... [at an object] adequate to the mind and will."[7]

Immersing oneself in *The Book of Divine Consolation* also brings the reader into the rich sensory imagery Blessed Angela found most apt for conveying her own experience. "I see those eyes, and that face so gracious and so pleasing, which embraceth and draweth my soul unto itself with infinite assurance. And that which proceeds from those eyes and that face is nothing else save that Good of which I spake before and which I beheld darkly.... And it is that Good wherein I delight so greatly that I can in no wise speak of it."[8]

After a life of ravishing happiness along with excruciating pain, Blessed Angela left this world in 1309 surrounded by her faithful spiritual sons and daughters.

The onset of the mystical life of Blessed Angela came with a pilgrimage. Many contemporary Catholics find that their way with the Lord intensifies after making a special pilgrimage to the site of an apparition or some other holy place. One of the first acts enjoined on Angela after her conversion was to divest herself of her possessions. We might ponder the amount of time we spend in such activities as buying and servicing our worldly goods or watching television. Diminishing these distractions would leave more time and interior space for contemplation and for works of love.

THE PERSONAL LOVE OF GOD

Sometimes we lapse into thinking that God loves each of us not so much personally but just as one more example of a human being he created. Yet the loving parents of a large family can truthfully say to each child, "I love you best." For their love for each one is not diminished by being given to all their children. In the spirit of this analogy, we can best understand the locutions of God to Angela about his intense personal love for her.

As I went unto St. Francis [to his church in Assisi] I prayed by the way. And amongst other prayers, I did ask the Blessed Francis that he would implore God for me, that I might serve well his Order... and that he would obtain for me the grace that I might feel somewhat of Christ.... Now when I was come to that place which lieth between Spello and the narrow road which leadeth upward unto Assisi ... it was said unto me:

"Thou hast prayed unto My servant Francis, and

I have not willed to send thee another messenger. I am the Holy Spirit, who am come unto thee to bring thee such consolation as thou hast never before tasted.... I will bear thee company and will speak with thee all the way.... My daughter who art sweet unto Me, my daughter who art My temple: My beloved daughter, do thou love Me, for I do greatly love thee and much more than thou lovest Me.... I love thee better than any other who is in the valley of Spoleto.... If there were today any person who loved Me more, much more would I do for him."[9]

Again He said unto me: "My beloved and my bride, love thou Me! All thy life, thy eating and drinking and sleeping and all that thou dost is pleasing unto Me, if only thou lovest Me."[10]

Then He departed with great gentleness; not suddenly, but slowly and gradually. Of the words which He spake unto me, the greatest are these: "Oh my daughter, who art sweeter to Me than I am unto thee, temple of My delight, thou dost possess the ring of My love and art promised unto Me, so that henceforth thou shalt never leave Me. The blessing of the Father, the Son, and the Holy Spirit be upon thee and thine understanding."

Then cried my soul, "If only Thou wilt not leave me, I will commit no mortal sin!"

And He answered me, "That say I not unto thee."[11]

Again He said unto me: "Infinite is the love which I bear thee, but I do not reveal it unto thee—yea, I do even conceal it."

When He told me that He concealed much love, because I was not able to bear it, my soul answered: "If Thou art God omnipotent, make Thou me able to bear it."

Then He made answer finally and said: "If I were to do as thou askest, thou wouldst have here all that thou desirest, and wouldst no longer hunger after Me. For this reason will I not grant thy request, for I desire that in this world thou shouldst hunger and long after Me and shouldst ever be eager to find Me."[12]

THE GOODNESS OF HOLY POVERTY

When our minds are cluttered with possessive concerns about things or persons, we are not free to experience all that God wishes for us to taste of the heavenly kingdom.

Thee do I praise, oh God my delight, for upon Thy Cross have I made my bed, and instead of a pillow have I found poverty, instead of repose have I found suffering and contempt, for upon this bed was He born, He lived, and laid Him down to die.[13]

In the midst of a dialogue with Christ, Angela is praying for her spiritual sons: For He Hath called and chosen them in order that they may think, see, and speak according unto His will.... Thus was it set forth and told unto me:

"Those who love My poverty, suffering, contempt are My lawful sons and Mine elect, whose thoughts are fixed on My Passion and Death, for here and nowhere else is found salvation and true life for all; wherefore are these and none others My lawful sons."[14]

In the midst of a long dialogue about Christ's reparation for the sins of the world, Angela heard the Lord speak these words: "Because of the sin of thy wealth, wherewith thou hast done evil by acquiring, wrongfully spending, and saving it, I have been poor, possessing neither palace, nor house, nor hut, wherein I might be born or where I might dwell during my lifetime. … My blood and My life have I given unto perverse and sinful men; nothing whatsoever have I kept for Myself, but in life and death have I desired to be and to remain poor forever."[15]

DOUBTS, FEARS, AND REASSURANCE

Viewing herself always as a sinner, our saintly woman mystic is continually in need of reassurance. Otherwise she would consider it impossible that she should be the recipient of so much love from God. Let us meditate on the words of consolation she received and apply them to ourselves, believing that God values the love that is in our hearts in spite of all that is still disordered and weak in our lives.

Wherefore hast Thou such love and joy in me, who

am hateful, inasmuch as I have offended Thee all the days of my life?

To this did He make answer: "So great is the love I bear thee that I no more remember thy sins, albeit Mine eyes do see them; for in thee have I much treasure."[16]

Then I besought Him that He would give me some tangible sign, something which I could see; such as putting a candle into my hand, or a precious stone ... promising Him that I would show it unto no person save unto whom He should desire.

Then He replied: "This sign that thou seekest is one that would only give thee great joy when thou didst behold or touch it, but it would not free thee from doubt, and thou mightest be deceived by that sign. Therefore will I give thee another sign, better than the one thou seekest, and which will be for ever with thee, and in thy soul thou shalt always feel it. The sign shall be this: thou shalt be ever fervent in love, and the love and the enlightened knowledge of God shall be ever with thee and in thee. This shall be a certain sign unto thee that I am He, because none save I can do this."[17]

"Oh Master,... never have I loved Thee saving deceitfully. I have served Thee with lies and I have never desired to draw nigh unto Thee in very truth for fear lest I might feel those burdens which Thou didst feel and bear for my sake...."

I did hear Him say unto me, "I know thy soul more intimately than it knoweth itself."[18]

Then were all my sins shown unto my soul, and I perceived that each member had its special spiritual infirmity.... "Oh Lord, Master and Physician of eternal health! Oh my God, forasmuch as by only showing forth unto Thee my infirmities and diseases Thou hast consented to heal me, and because, oh Lord, I am very sick and have no part in me that is not corrupt and defiled, I, wretched that I am, will show Thee, oh Lord, all mine infirmities and all the sins of all my members and of all the parts of my soul and body!" Then did I begin and point them all out, saying "Oh Lord,... look upon mine head and see how ofttimes I have adorned it with the emblems of pride, how I have many times deformed it by curling and braiding my hair.... Look, oh Lord, upon my wretched eyes, full of uncleanness and envy!"

And when He had hearkened thereunto with great patience, the Lord Jesus Christ did gladly and joyfully make answer that He had healed these things one after another.... He said: "Fear not, My daughter, neither do thou despair; for even wert thou tainted a thousand deadly diseases... yet could I give thee a medicine whereby thou mightest be healed of everything.... For these infirmities have I given satisfaction and done penance. I suffered the most grievous pain inasmuch as My hair was plucked out and my head pierced by sharp thorns.... For thine eyes, with which thou hast looked at vain and hurtful things and hast delighted in gazing at many things which were opposed unto God, have I given satisfaction, shedding copious and bitter tears from My eyes which were veiled and filled with blood...."[19]

THE CENTRALITY OF THE PASSION

As is the case with all Christian mystics, the Passion is a central theme for contemplative prayer. It is by uniting ourselves to the sufferings of our Lord that we take courage in accepting unavoidable sufferings in our own lives. More intimately, it is by loving Christ in his pain that we receive it as a gift of love for us—a sign of the unconditional completeness of his desire to help us come into the fullness of his promises.

Again after this it pleased Him to make me understand more things concerning His passion than I had ever hitherto heard related.... Therefore did my soul then cry aloud, saying: "Holy Mary, mother of Him who is thus afflicted, give me something of this Passion of the Son of God, for thou hast seen more of it than hath any other saint. Thou hast seen Him with the eyes both of thy body and thy mind, and most intently hast thou observed Him, because thou hast loved Him more than all."[20]

During her contemplation of the Passion, Blessed Angela heard Jesus say: "Ye shall have the blessing which I shall give at the last judgment, inasmuch as ye did not repulse Me when I came unto Mine own place, as did My persecutors, but of your compassion did receive Me into the lodging of your hearts as a desolate pilgrim; when I hanged naked upon the Cross, hungry, thirsty, and sick, and pierced by nails, ye did suffer with Me in My death and desired to be in all things My companions.... For if upon the Cross I did pray unto My Father with tears and cries for those who crucified and tormented Me, excusing them... what shall I say for you, who have had compassion upon Me and have been My faithful companions...."[21]

The Crucified One spake further unto me and said: "When these My sons, who through sin have departed from My kingdom and made themselves sons of the devil, do return unto the Father, He hath great joy of them and showeth them His exceeding great delight in their return. So great is the Father's joy at their conversion that He bestoweth on them supernatural grace, the which He giveth not unto virgins who through sin have not departed from Him. And this He doth because of the boundless love which He beareth them.... Whosoever desireth to find grace must not lift his eyes from the Cross, whether I do grant and permit him to live in joy, or whether he live in sorrow."[22]

3

Saint Gertrude the Great
(1256–1301)

*Let the desires and prayers of my heart sing jubilantly
unto Thee, and Thy gifts of so many graces chant Thy
praises. Let the groans and sighs of my sad sojourning
on this earth sing jubilantly unto Thee, and let my
expectation and patience bless Thee as I await my long-
deferred hope which is Thyself, O my God.*[1]

✠ ✠ ✠

S T. GERTRUDE THE GREAT was one of the most influential of woman mystics, unfortunately not as
often read today as in the past. As in the case of St.
Hildegard, her family sent her to the monastery as a
child—in this case the Abbey at Helfta in Germany.

At this Benedictine monastery which became a
renowned center of culture and piety, Gertrude
received an education in Latin, philosophy, and
literature. Her days were spent in chanting the
Liturgy of the Hours and in spinning wool. Although her writing is refined and poetical, Ger-

trude was also gifted with such great prudence that she was soon given a leadership role which she executed amidst great difficulty for forty years.

The advent of Gertrude's mystical prayer took place in 1281 when Christ suddenly appeared to her and said that he, himself, would direct her into a more supernatural life. The visions given to St. Gertrude after this led to the stigmata in 1284 and also the reception in her heart of the wound of love.[2]

Gertrude was especially devoted to the Passion, the Holy Eucharist, and to the Sacred Heart, which was revealed to her as well as to one of her mentors, St. Mechtild. The most well known of her writings is now called *The Messenger of Divine Loving Kindness.*[3] The more recent English translation entitled *The Exercises of Saint Gertrude*[4] consists of her spiritual direction for her sisters.

St. Gertrude's writings fit into a tradition called "bridal mysticism," following in the direction set out by St. Bernard of Clairvaux. She sees herself as a spouse of Christ, similar to the bride of the Song of Songs. The particular version of such bridal union in the spirituality of Gertrude is flavored by the purity of her heart, the simplicity of her state of life embraced so early as a young girl, and a passionate desire to witness to the beauty of God's ways. Gertrude died in 1301 surrounded by her most loving community of nuns.

It is characteristic of women to live primarily for

love. How sad, then, if a woman does not find a way to adore God with love and to experience his love in return with heartfelt joy! Many Catholic women fear the sweet sentimentality of the beautiful writings of women mystics of the type of St. Gertrude. However, if we release ourselves and get in touch with our own yearning for love, we can let our souls be carried by the music of intimate prayer. Then our hearts will soften and our lips sing a new song unto the Lord.

LITURGICAL MEDITATIONS

The most characteristic feature of St. Gertrude's writings is the way she intermingles her own prayers with liturgical and sacramental texts.

Concerning renewal of baptismal vows: O most loving Jesus, protect me beneath the shadow of Thy hand; let Thy right hand sustain me. Open unto me the door of Thy love, that having been dedicated with the seal of Thy wisdom, I may in truth be free from all earthly desire, serve Thee with joy in Thy holy Church according to the sweet odor of Thy precepts, and daily advance from strength unto strength. Amen.[5]

To accompany morning prayer: Unto me, O Love, O God, the vision of Thee is day most radiant, that one day in Thy courts which is better than a thousand elsewhere, that one day after which sigheth this soul of mine redeemed unto Thyself by Thee.

Come, when wilt Thou satisfy me with the sweetness of Thy glorious face? My soul longeth and fainteth after the richness of Thy delights. Behold, I have chosen and preferred to be a poor handmaid in the house of my God, that I may approach unto the refreshment of Thy all-beauteous face.[6]

Meditating at Vespers on the text, "If any man loves me, he will keep my word, and my Father will love him, and we will come to him and will make our abode with him" (John 14:23), Gertrude prayed: The excess of Thy goodness obliges me to believe that the sight of my faults rather moves Thee to fear Thou wilt see me perish than to excite Thine anger, making me know that Thy patience in supporting my defects until now, with so much goodness, is greater than the sweetness with which Thou didst bear with the perfidious Judas during Thy mortal life; and although my mind takes pleasure in wandering after and distracting itself with perishable things, yet, after some hours, after some days, and, alas! I must add, after whole weeks, when I return into my heart, I find Thee there; so that I cannot complain that Thou hast left me even for a moment....[7]

THE JOY OF THE BRIDE-SOUL

The following prayers reflect the very graceful and feminine charm of Gertrude's intimate manner of prayer.

Ah! Cement me to Thee, O true love. I offer Thee my chastity because Thou art altogether dulcet and

pleasant, my spouse full of delight. I vow obedience
to Thee because Thy fatherly charity allures me,
Thy loving kindness and gentleness attract me. In
observing Thy will, I tie myself to Thee because
clinging to Thee is lovable above everything....[8]

Come, O Love, O God, Thou alone art all my love in
verity. Thou art my dearest Salvation, all my hope
and my joy, my supreme and surpassing Good. In
the morning I will stand before Thee, my God, and
will contemplate Thee, my dearest Love, because
Thou art pure delightsomeness and sweetness eternal. Thou art the thirst of my heart; Thou art all the
sufficiency of my spirit. The more I taste Thee, the
more I hunger; the more I drink, the more I thirst.[9]

Come, admit me unto the intimacy of Thy charity.
Behold, my heart burneth already for the kiss of
Thy love. Open unto me the privy chamber of Thy
fair love. Behold, my soul thirsteth for the embrace
of most secret union with Thee.[10]

In weariness close to death: O Thou living God, the
inflow of Thy burning love draweth back into Thy
bosom all beings which have ever flowed forth from
Thee; but all my life, alas! is lost, withered, and
brought to naught. Come, O God of my life, let my
life grow green again in Thee, put forth new flowers, and regain the strength to bear its due fruit. O
my Beloved, by the exalted innocence and flawless
sanctity of Thy life, wash away all the foulness of my
corrupt life, that my life may no longer be with me,

but by the force of Thy burning love may be wholly transported into Thee. Then in the hour of my death I shall rejoice, O my true Life! to find myself in Thee.... Thou alone art the refuge of my soul. Come, grant that I may grow faint with love for Thee, die of desire for Thee, praise Thee with jubilation, and be for all eternity enkindled with the blazing fire of Thy charity. Amen.[11]

PRAYERS TO THE SACRED HEART

These prayers indicate the way Jesus began to reveal the mysteries of his Sacred Heart to mystics long before this devotion became so popular in the church of our century.

Come, open unto me the portal of salvation of Thy most beloved Heart. Behold, I no longer have my own heart with me, but Thou, O my dearest Treasure, dost keep it with Thee in Thy closed chamber.[12]

O Heart, fountain of sweetness!... Give me to drink unworthy as I am, of the wine of Thy comfort; in Thy divine charity raise up the ruins of my spirit, and out of Thy superabundance of charity atone for all the beggary and neediness of my soul.[13]

O eternal sweetness of my soul, Thou who alone art the Beloved of my heart, Thy face is all lovely and Thy Heart all inviting; but my thoughts, alas! go wandering far from Thee. Come, O God of my heart, gather together my scattered mental powers and fix them upon Thyself. O my Beloved, by the pure intention of Thy most holy thoughts and the ardent love of Thy transpierced Heart, wash away all the guilt of my evil thoughts and my sinful heart, that Thy most bitter passion may be my shady bower in death, and Thy Heart, broken by love, my everlasting dwelling place....[14]

Let Thy Divine and most sweet Heart, which, in the hour of Thy death, love did pierce for my sake, sing jubilantly unto Thee. Let Thy most loving and most faithful Heart, into which the lance did open a way for me, that my heart might enter and rest therein, sing jubilantly unto Thee. Let this Heart most sweet, the sole refuge of my earthly sojourning, which ever watcheth over me with such kindness, and which will never rest in its thirst for me until it taketh me eternally unto itself, sing jubilantly unto Thee.

Let the incomparable heart and soul of the most glorious Virgin Mary, whom Thou didst choose as Thy Mother for my salvation and advantage, that her motherly clemency might ever avail me, sing jubilantly unto Thee.[15]

4

Hadewijch of Belgium
(Thirteenth Century)

O Love, were I but love,
And could I but love you, Love, with love!
O Love, for love's sake, grant that I,
Having become love, may know Love wholly as Love![1]

✠ ✠ ✠

A BELGIAN MYSTIC, better known to lovers of religious poetry than to Christian contemplatives, is Hadewijch the Beguine. She was a member of a community of devout women called Beguines, who lived together without vows in apostolic poverty. Their way of life called for much prayer as well as tending the poor and the ill.

Little is known of the happenings of Hadewijch's life. What appears certain is that she was of the higher classes, well-educated in Latin and the liberal arts, along with Scripture and Catholic tradition.

Although some questioned her unusual modes of expression, investigations did not lead to censure or condemnation. In fact, her writings were much admired by such fourteenth-century lights as Ruysbroeck. These writings were subsequently lost and then rediscovered in Brussels in 1838 by scholars studying old medieval texts. They consist of letters, poems, and accounts of her visions.

Hadewijch was the spiritual guide of her community. At one point, however, envy and misunderstandings led to exile. Her poetry reflects the great grief inflicted by these happenings.

The spirituality of Hadewijch falls clearly into the contemplative tradition called "bridal mysticism." God is experienced as the consummate lover, as depicted in the spiritual interpretation of the Song of Songs. Her arresting visions and poetic images revolve around themes that could be related to these perennial queries of lament:

- If God's love for us is perfect, why do we experience it as so changeable—sometimes present, sometimes hidden?
- Does the feeling of abandonment by God signify punishment for our own failings or only the mystery of God's unknowable designs for us?
- If intense religious yearning leaves us sometimes in despair, should we flee to the safer path of vocal and meditative prayer?

What is most striking are Hadewijch's descriptions of the interior agony that accompanies her ardent love for Christ as her spouse. Her poems about these sorrows will especially appeal to readers of a similarly passionate temperament, but may also help others to understand the logic of what transpires within the hearts of their more fiery sisters and brothers.

I have chosen Hadewijch's poem-prayers for this book because they are more beautiful and require less surrounding text for understanding. Whenever a part of a poem might be a bit cryptic, I have appended a short explanation in italics. Hadewijch uses feminine pronouns for Divine Love, likening the soul to a knight who is being conquered by a mysterious damsel.

Perhaps one of the greatest reasons why many Christians remain only half-saints is the pain of living continually stretched between time and eternity. We find it so much easier to make a morning offering, visit the church, read Scripture, and try to avoid the worst sins. Indeed, we can easily pride ourselves on being better than most other people because of such external practices.

We soon tire of the effort of trying to abide in love every moment of the day by continual dialogue with God and care for one's neighbor. Hadewijch's laments offer little comfort to those who have grown weary from such strain. They are more helpful to those who need to know more of the landmarks of the "road less traveled," the road of total commitment. Such sojourners will welcome a sister who comes along singing the songs of the Lord in a strange land.

THE PARADOX OF LOVE

A paradox is a statement that appears to be contradictory yet is nevertheless true. For example, a person may say "I love you, but I also hate you." Even though such a sentiment seems impossible, it can nonetheless be real in some senses of the words love and hate. To experience divine love as paradoxical is to realize that far from being a simple bath of warmth, God's love is more like a magnet pulling us up a high mountain often against our will.

Oh, if my Beloved let me obtain what is lovable in
    love,
Love would not be completely exhausted by it,
And so there would be no joy but a delusion;
And if this happened it would be a pity.
O may God make noble spirits understand
What harm would come of it.[2]

Love is greater than warm cuddles. If we received only God's comfort we would be in the delusion that this was all he wanted for us—instead of stretching for the real breadth and depth of God.

What is sweetest in Love is her tempestuousness....
to lose one's way in her is to touch her close at
    hand;
to die of hunger for her is to feed and taste....
Wordlessness is her most beautiful utterance;
imprisonment by her is total release....
Her tender care enlarges our wounds....
Her promises are all seductions;
Her adornments are all undressing....[3]

Love seems to promise blissful fulfillment on earth, but instead the mystical experience of love is really a stripping, releasing us from all else and leaving us still unsatisfied in this life.

O powerful, wonderful Love,
You who can conquer all with wonder!
Conquer me, so that I may conquer you,
In your unconquered Power.
In the past I knew this conquering:
In conquering there is a knowledge
That always oppressed me most sorely.

But you are still, Love, what you always were:
They who are with you in all know this.
I admit it; to spare oneself is useless.
The misfortune that barred my way
Was my not yet knowing
And not yet loving this work
By which fidelity will help me attain the end.[4]

In moments of ecstasy, it seems that we can gain God in one fell swoop, but this yields swiftly to the bitter knowledge of exile from ecstasy into normal existence. However, one gradually learns that there is no way to spare oneself these emotional swings, but that it is precisely fidelity to the daily works of love God asks that leads to truly conquering.

DIVINE PROVIDENCE IS UNFATHOMABLE

We would like to be able to predict love's visitations. Since God is a living God and not our puppet, of course, his

*times will not be our times. Since we cannot know the whys
and wherefores of his visitations, we would do better to surrender ourselves to following Christ and let him take care of
when to give us joys, exterior or interior. As Hadewijch
teaches: "Serve nobly, wish for nothing else, and fear nothing else and let Love freely take care of herself! For Love
rewards to the full, even though she often comes late. Let no
doubt or disappointment ever turn you away from perform-
ing acts of virtue."[5]*

Alas, Love, your wrath and your favor
We cannot distinguish—
Your high will and our debt,
Why you come, or why you fly.
For you can give, in response to small service,
Your sweet splendours in great clarity;
But for small faults this seems withheld,
And then you give blows and bitter death.[6]

Alas, Love, if you play the niggard with me,
I vow I will play the niggard with you!
I wonder how it comes to pass
That you stay a great distance off?
You are far from me, and I am near you;
Therefore I live continually in the sad season.[7]

Alas, Love! who will raise you in himself to your full
     height,
So that you, all that you are, may draw him?
Who will struggle through the deep valleys,
The high mountains, the wide fields,

With deep humility in new ardor,
With confidence in high delight,
Strong in combat?
Help quickly in this, O Love; there is need, it is high
   time![8]

THE PROMISE OF ETERNAL LOVE

*We would like to sink to a lower level of consciousness to
avoid the painfulness of longing for God and not being
able to dwell with him now. What justifies the pain of the
pilgrimage and gives us the courage to continue on the
more intimate mystical path is the promise of eternal fullness.*

We find valleys in Love's heights;
Whoever finds heights in these valleys
Is of rich insight.
Since Love first commanded torment for me,
He who gives me any other commands torments
   me:
I place torment before all profit.
For I know this is the best life for me,
Since Love has commanded me to wander about
In the climb to the highest summits.
May God now come to our assistance![9]

Fortunate is he who can wait
Until Love gives him all in exchange for his all....
I have abandoned myself wholly to Love.
But woe has treated me all too harshly....

To stray after Love without knowing where,
Be it in darkness or in daylight,
In wrath or in lovingness: Were Love
To give her consolation unmistakably,
This would satisfy the exiled soul.[10]

May God give good success to all lovers, as is fitting.
Though I and many others have so little
part in Love,
They who know her fully give all for all.
She gives herself wholly to whom she pleases.
He who was empowered always attained her.
What use is it for anyone to fear
What must invariably happen?
All her blows are good.
But it takes a warrior to keep up the fight![11]

5

Saint Birgitta of Sweden
(1303–1373)

O Jesus, only begotten Son of the most high Father, splendor and figure of His substance, remember Thou didst commend Thy spirit to Thy Father, saying, "Into Thy hands, O Lord, I commend my spirit!" And then, with lacerated body and broken heart, with a loud cry, the breasts of Thy mercy exposed, Thou didst expire to redeem us. By this precious death, I beseech Thee, O King of saints, comfort me to resist the devil, the world and the flesh and blood, that, dead to the world, I may live in Thee; and in the last hour of my departure, receive Thou my exiled wandering spirit as it returns to Thee.[1]

✠ ✠ ✠

IN 1303 A SEVENTH CHILD was born to one of the leading noble families in Finsta, Sweden. During the night of this birth, "the parish priest… was praying devoutly, when he saw as it were a bright cloud, and in the cloud sat a virgin holding a book in her hand. He marveled greatly what this might mean. Then the virgin said to him: 'A daughter has been born to Master Birger, and her wondrous voice shall be heard all over the world.'"[2] They named her Birgitta, which means "hard, bright and exalted."[3]

Both parents were devout. They taught their children how to pray in love of the Lord. One evening when Birgitta was eleven years old, she heard a sermon on the Passion preached by a Dominican friar. "That same evening as she prayed before the Crucifix, suddenly the room was filled with an ineffable light, and Christ appeared to Birgitta pointing to His five wounds. Only slowly she could utter, 'Oh, my dearest Lord, who has ill-treated You so?' And Christ sadly answered, 'All they who forgot Me and despise My love.' At this moment Birgitta felt as if a gryphon's beak plunged into her heart."[4]

The image of the gryphon in those days referred to Christ as the bird of prey who chooses only the finest hearts. The young girl was never to forget this vision as she grew in grace, beauty, and learning. As the daughter of the chief lawmaker of the region, Birgitta's education was considerable. She studied Latin, theology, philosophy, and church history with a leading scholar and suggested to her professor that the Bible be translated into Swedish.

In her piety Birgitta was especially influenced by St. Bernard. Although she wished to become a nun, she willingly obeyed her parents and married Prince Ulf of Nericia at the age of fourteen. This happy marriage resulted in eight children, one of whom was St. Catherine of Sweden. Birgitta herself was a Third Order Franciscan.

From their early youth, Birgitta instructed her children in the Christian life. Bringing the girls along with her to the hospital she had built, this servant of God proved to them that it was no shame for a rich family to tend the wounds of the poor, feed them, and wash their feet. In addition to her charitable deeds, Birgitta continually worked for reform of the laws in favor of true justice.

While outwardly living the courtly life of the time, Birgitta wore a hair shirt underneath her heavy brocade dresses. She even kept a bitter herb in her mouth to chew on in order to avoid the gossiping so prevalent in society!

As the noble classes were becoming more and more corrupt, Birgitta often felt called to exercise the ministry of prophecy in correcting worldly patterns of the day. Confronting King Magnus, she proclaimed: "You know, O King... three sins hold sway in this kingdom: gluttony, the lust of the flesh and the pride of life."[5]

In other prophecies, Birgitta spoke of the unnatural forms of sexual intercourse which had spread from the influence of other European countries. The predicted calamities could be prevented if the King would lead a reform of morals. Not one to only talk without seeking concrete solutions, Birgitta made it a practice to visit houses of prostitution. She sought women who might be apt for religious life, and even provided the dowry for those who preferred marriage.

During this time Christ appeared to Birgitta and ordered her to found a monastery at Vadstena. Called the Order of the Holy Saviour, sixty nuns, with priests, brothers, and lay sisters to help, were all headed by an abbess. The nuns were contemplative and ascetical, while the priests had an active apostolic vocation.

At age forty Birgitta was widowed. "When I buried my husband," she wrote, "I buried all my earthly love with him, for though I loved him as my own soul, I would not for a penny buy back his life against the will of God. As long as I kept this wedding ring it was like a burden to me, because I remembered my lost joy. But now my soul will love God only, and therefore I will forget both my ring and my husband."[6]

After Birgitta had for some years obediently followed the Holy Spirit's command to remain among the Swedish nobility, Christ told her that she must journey to Rome to reconcile the pope in Avignon with the emperor. "Go to Rome... and stay in Rome until you see the Pope and Emperor together, and then you will proclaim My words to them."[7]

This story is told of Birgitta's response to the news of the death in a Swedish convent of one of her daughters who was a nun:

> "Oh, Lord Jesus Christ, I bless Thee, because Thou hast called her before the world could ensnare her." And she arose at once and went into the chapel, and those who stood outside heard her sighing and weeping much.... Then Christ

appeared to her and said: "Woman, why weepest thou?" But she answered: "Lord, I do not weep because my daughter is dead…. But I weep because I did not bring her up according to Thy commandments… because I gave her examples of pride, and because I did not chastise her as I should have done when she erred." Christ replied: "And for the sake of thy love and for thy good will thy daughter has now been crowned in heaven with the crown of glory."[8]

While in Rome Birgitta also wrote her prophetic *Revelations*, which included details about future events in church history. These writings became quite well known and were influential in changing matters for the better. She lived to see the emperor, Charles IV, accompany Pope Urban back from France to Rome. Many times it was necessary for her to scold various popes for their weaknesses. The Archbishop of Naples once assembled all the leaders and doctors of theology to hear the proclamations of Birgitta.

On pilgrimage to the Holy Land, Birgitta received many revelations from the Virgin Mary concerning such mysteries as the Immaculate Conception and the Assumption. Her visions of the Passion especially influenced Catholic art, music, and literature. Among the most well known of the paintings reflective of mystical visions of Birgitta are the Avignon Pietà and Grunewald's "Crucifixion."

Known as the Sybil of the North and the Angel of

Rome, Birgitta died in Rome at age seventy. Her own daughter, Catherine, worked on her canonization. The ecumenical interest of followers of St. Birgitta stems from a Revelation (VI, 77) "that time will come when there shall be one flock and one Shepherd, one faith and one clear knowledge of God." Popular devotions based on prayers from her visions are widespread in the Catholic world.

The fundamental spirituality that emerges from the study of *Revelations* is rather simple, especially as compared to the more developed systems of such mystics as St. Teresa of Avila. Birgitta's writings reflect her profound wonder at the reality of the mysteries of the lives of the Virgin Mary and the Lord Jesus Christ. By centering the soul on these historical facts in their specific sensory details, the heart is moved from coldness to fiery love.

Some Christians who feel drawn toward contemplation fear that such a path may alienate them from the battle for justice in the world. The life of St. Birgitta indicates how a life devoted to serving the needs of the poor and insisting on the righteousness of leaders is nourished by interior prayer. In fact, only because St. Birgitta was so respected for her holiness were her plans for the improvement of the world taken seriously.

Does her example suggest prayer as simply a means for attaining power? Quite the contrary. It was because of her selfless devotion to God that Birgitta was given the power to use her noble status for the promotion of true good. Such deep devotion to God must be nourished by much time spent at the foot of the cross.

IN HONOR OF THE BLESSED VIRGIN MARY

Some of the most familiar images of biblical events enshrined in these prayers were popularized through the influence of St. Birgitta's writings.

Blessed and venerated be thou, my Lady Virgin Mary, most holy Mother of God, Whose noblest creature thou art, and Who was never so loved as by thee, O glorious Lady....

Blessed be thou, my Lady Virgin Mary, who didst constantly feel the body of Christ, created of thy blessed body, grow and move in thy womb till the time of His glorious Nativity; Whom thou before all others didst touch with thy sacred hands, wrap up in clothes, and according to the prophecy, didst lay in a manger and didst maternally nurture....

Blessed be thou, my Lady Virgin Mary, who didst beforehand know that thy Son was to be arrested, and didst afterward, with thy blessed eyes, mournfully see Him bound and scourged, crowned with thorns and fastened naked to the Cross....

Rejoice, my most worthy Lady Virgin Mary, that the very moment thy Son rose from the dead, He wished it to be known to thee, His most Blessed Mother, because He at once appeared in person to thee, then showed to others that He, Who underwent death in His living body, was risen from the dead....

Rejoice, my Lady Virgin Mary, and let the whole earth rejoice with thy joy, that thy Son permitted thee to remain many years in this world after His Ascension, to console His friends and strengthen them in faith, to help the needy, and sagely to counsel the Apostles....

Exult, O Mother of God, glorious Lady Virgin Mary, that thou didst deserve to see thy body quickened after death, assumed with thy soul with angelic honors to heaven, and that thou didst see with exultation thy glorious Son, God with humanity, to be the most just judge of all men, and rewarder of good works....

Blessed be thou, O my Lady Virgin Mary, that every faithful creature praises the Trinity for thee, because thou art His most worthy creature, who dost most promptly obtain pardon for wretched souls, who art the most faithful advocate for all sinners.[9]

IN HONOR OF OUR LORD JESUS CHRIST

When reading these prayers of St. Birgitta, try to picture in your own mind what she is describing in relation to your own physical and mental pain—past, present, or dreaded. In this way you may receive some of the consolation experienced by those in excruciating pain in the hospital at

Isenheim who viewed the famous paintings of Grunewald based exactly on Birgitta's Revelations.

O Lord God, forgive me my sins for the sake of Thy bitter pain and for Thy love of the race of man. O Lord Jesus, Who was taken captive by enemies, have mercy upon me. O Lord Jesus, Who stoodest bound to the stake, have mercy upon me. O Lord Jesus, Who was without guilt and was judged by heartless men, have mercy upon me. O Lord Jesus, Thou Who was robbed of Thy garments, and clad in the raiment of mockery, have mercy upon us. O Lord Jesus Who was so cruelly torn that Thy bones could be seen and there was not a whole spot upon Thee, have mercy upon me. O Lord Jesus, Thou Who was stretched upon the Cross, as a bird of prey is stretched with nails upon the door of a barn, have mercy upon me.[10]

O Jesus, heavenly physician, remember the languor, lividness and pain which Thou didst suffer on the lofty scaffold on the Cross, torn in all Thy limbs, not one of which remained in its right state, so that Thy pain was like no other, for from the sole of Thy foot to the top of Thy head there was no soundness in Thee. And yet, regardless of all pains, Thou didst piously pray to Thy Father for Thy enemies.... By this mercy and in remembrance of that pain, grant that my memory of Thy most bitter Passion be a full remission of all my sins.[11]

O Jesus, amiable king and most desirable friend, remember the sorrow Thou hadst, when Thou didst hang naked and wretched on the Cross, and all Thy friends and enemies stood under Thee, and Thou didst find no comforter except Thy beloved Mother. ... I beseech Thee, merciful Jesus, by the sword of grief which then pierced Thy soul, have compassion on me in all my tribulations and afflictions, bodily and spiritual, and give me comfort at the hour of my death.[12]

O Jesus, most profound abyss of mercy, I beseech Thee by the depth of Thy wounds, which pierced Thy vitals and the marrow of Thy bones, raise me from the depth of sin in which I am plunged, and hide me in the hollow of Thy wounds, from the face of Thy wrath, till Thy anger pass away.[13]

O sweet Jesus, true and fruitful vine, remember the overflowing and abundant effusion of blood, which poured in torrents, like wine pressed from the grape, when on the press of the Cross Thou didst tread alone, and Thy side having been opened with a lance, Thou didst pour forth to us blood and water, so that not the least drop remained in Thee; and at last Thou was suspended on high like a bundle of myrrh, Thy delicate flesh faded, the moisture of Thy members and the marrow of Thy bones dried up. By this most bitter Passion and the effusion of Thy precious blood, I pray Thee, receive my soul in the agony of my death.[14]

6

Blessed Julian of Norwich
(1343–1423)

Then our courteous Lord shows himself to the soul most merrily and with a glad expression. With a friendly welcome, as if the soul had been in pain and imprisoned, he says sweetly, "My darling, I am glad you have come to me. In all this misery I have ever been with you. Now you see my loving, and we are made one in bliss."[1]

✠ ✠ ✠

LITTLE IS KNOWN OF THE YOUTH of the lady who was called Julian when she became an anchorite at the church of St. Julian. Her writings indicate such literary skill, in spite of her denials, that it is surmised that she must have come from the upper classes. We do have evidence that Julian lived in fourteenth-century England and was born in Norfolk.

As a child she was unhappy and prayed for an early death. In the midst of an illness, however, young Julian received such clear visions of the

Passion that she was led to choose the secluded life. She subsequently spent much of her time in prayer and in reading spiritual books in the city of Norwich, a famous theological center during her times.

Her visions—which Julian called "showings"—took place after a particular personal prayer, which led not only to severe sufferings but also to fulsome joys. She recounts her experience in this manner:

> These revelations were showed to a simple uneducated creature living in mortal flesh in the year of our Lord 1373, on the eighth day of May.
>
> This creature had desired beforehand three gifts of God by his grace. The first was to enter into the spirit of Christ's passion. The second was bodily sickness in youth. The third was to have from God the gift of three wounds... the wound of true contrition, the wound of natural compassion, and the wound of full-hearted longing for God.[2]

Julian was considered to be the first woman of letters in the history of England. Her writings are characterized by a mixture of the feminine, homey imagery, and high philosophy. They are delicate, beautiful, and full of surprises. A typical example is this excerpt: "Our Lord gave me a spiritual insight into the unpretentious manner of his loving. I saw that for us he is everything that is good, comforting and helpful; he is our clothing, who, for love, wraps us up, holds us close; he entirely encloses us for tender love, so that he may never leave us, since he is the source of all good things for us...."[3]

Some feminists consider Julian to be a prototype of radical thought. Her writings indeed reveal a feminine mind struggling to reconcile her own experience with biblical revelation and with the teachings of the church. Like Augustine, she was not easily satisfied and begged God to answer her many questions.

Julian also used maternal imagery, describing Christ as "our mother entirely in everything.... A mother's service is nearest, readiest and surest. It is nearest because it is most natural. It is readiest because it is most loving. And it is surest because it is most true. This office no one but him alone might or could ever have performed to the full."[4] Like a mother, Jesus bears us in pain and is willing to die for our benefit.

However, it is one thing to believe that God contains everything good that is feminine and another to think of God as a goddess. This would be as if a child would praise his father for being as tender as a mother, and then suggest calling him "Mom." God is revealed in the Scriptures primarily as Father.

To the contrary, Julian specifically alludes to the need for fidelity to church teaching and tradition. "For a person by himself can frequently be broken... but the whole body of holy Church was never broken and never shall be, without end. Therefore it is a sure thing, a good thing, and a gracious thing to will meekly and powerfully to be fastened and joined to our mother, holy Church—that is Christ Jesus."[5]

And, again: "In all things I believe as holy Church believes, preaches and teaches."[6]

Very few formal prayers of petition appear in the writings of St. Julian. Instead we are regaled with evocative images coming from the infused prayer given her as "showings." Although she writes in a classical way about the sufferings of Christ, this English holy woman is most remembered for the joy that abounds in her most original sharings.

Do we meditate enough on the wonders of creation and the joys awaiting us in eternity? I think not. Too often we sink into melancholy because of the pain of this world. Like Julian of Norwich, let us allow God to sing his songs of hope in our hearts.

GOD'S DESIGNS

What is most delightful in the revelations of Julian are the sensory images the Holy Spirit uses to convey spiritual truths. She is especially gifted in seeing God's designs as shown in the analogies of nature.

He also showed me a little thing, the size of a hazelnut, lying in the palm of my hand. It was as round as a ball, as it seemed to me. I looked at it with the eyes of my understanding and thought, "What can this be?" My question was answered in general terms in this fashion: "It is everything that is made." I marveled how this could be, for it seemed to me that it might suddenly fall into nothingness, it was so small.

An answer for this was given to my understanding: "It lasts, and ever shall last, because God loves it. And in this fashion all things have their being by the grace of God.... It is necessary for us to know the littleness of creatures in order to reduce them to nothingness in our judgment, so that we may love and have the uncreated God. The reason we are not fully at ease in heart and soul is because we seek rest in these things that are so little and have no rest within them, and pay no attention to our God, who is Almighty, All-wise, All-good and the only real rest."[7]

An image taken from our digestive system: A man walks upright and his soul is enclosed in his body as in a beautiful purse. In time of necessity, the purse is opened and closed again, quite properly. And that it is God who does this work is shown where he says he comes down to us to the lowest part of our need, for he has no contempt for what he has made. Further, he does not disdain to serve us in the simplest requirements the nature of our body demands, for love of the soul he has made in his own likeness.[8]

Describing a vision of the crown of thorns on the head of Christ: The plenteousness of the bleeding is like the drops of water that fall from the eaves of the house after a great rainstorm; they fall so thick no man can count them with his human powers. As they spread over the forehead, the drops of blood were like herring scales in their roundness.[9]

GOD'S PROVIDENCE

What Christian has not questioned God's love in the light of all the evils and sufferings in the world! Here are some revelations made to Julian to console us.

Man sees some deeds as well done, and some deeds as evil, but our Lord does not see things that way.... I saw with full certainty that God never changes his purpose in the slightest degree, and never shall forever. Because there was nothing unknown to him in his rightful laws from eternity.... No kind of thing shall fail... for he made all things in the fullness of goodness. Therefore, the blessed Trinity is forever pleased in all his works. All this he showed me most blissfully, intending this to be understood! "I never take my hands off my works, and never shall forever. See! I lead all things to the end I ordained for them from eternity, by the same might, wisdom and love by which I made them. How should anything be amiss?"[10]

I often wondered why, by the great foreseeing wisdom of God, the beginning of sin had not been prevented, for then, I thought, all would have been well.... I mourned and sorrowed on its account without reason or discretion. But Jesus, who in this vision informed me of all I needed to know, answered in these words, saying, "Sin is necessary, but all shall be well, and all shall be well, and all manner of things shall be well."

... Pain is something for a time, as I see it, for it

purges us and makes us know ourselves and ask for mercy.... "All shall be well, and all shall be well, and all manner of things shall be well." These words were said most tenderly, showing no kind of blame assigned to me or to anyone who shall be saved. Consequently, it would be a most unnatural act for me to blame or wonder at God on account of my sin, seeing that he does not blame me for sin.[11]

JOY OF CHRISTIANS AND OF GOD HIMSELF

Julian tells us of a type of joy that is not only quiet exaltation but also sheer delight. And this joy is but a mirror of God's joy in our salvation.

I saw our Lord scorn [the devil's] malice and reduce his powerlessness to nothing, and he wills that we do the same thing. On account of this sight, I laughed loud and long, which made those who were around me laugh too, and their laughter was a pleasure to me....[12]

"It is a joy, a bliss, an endless delight to me that I ever suffered the passion for you."[13]

My understanding was lifted up into heaven, where I saw our Lord like a lord in his own house who has called all his valued servants and friends to a solemn feast. Then I saw the Lord... reign there, and he completely filled it with joy and mirth. He himself endlessly gladdens and solaces his valued friends most modestly and courteously with the marvelous melody of endless love in his own fair, blessed face. This glorious countenance of the godhead completely fills all heaven with joy and bliss.

God showed three degrees of bliss that every soul that has willingly served God in any degree on earth shall have in heaven.

The first is the gratitude full of honor that he shall receive from our Lord God [for his service to God during his life].... The second degree of bliss is that all the blessed creatures who are in heaven shall see that glorious thanking, and God shall make his service known to all who are in heaven.... The third degree of bliss is that it shall last forever, just as new and pleasing as it is when it is first received.[14]

7

Saint Catherine of Siena
(1347–1380)

Why did you so dignify us? With unimaginable love you looked upon your creatures within your very self, and you fell in love with us. So it was love that made you create us and give us being just so that we might taste your supreme eternal good. Then I see how by our sin we lost the dignity you had given us…. So you gave us your only-begotten Son, your Word…. We are your image, and now by making yourself one with us you have become our image, veiling your eternal divinity in the wretched cloud and dung heap of Adam. And why? For love! You, God, became human and we have been made divine! In the name of this unspeakable love, then, I beg you—I would force you even!—to have mercy on your creatures."[1]

✠ ✠ ✠

S T. CATHERINE WAS not only a great mystic but also a Doctor of the Church.[2] I love her most for the intensity of her dialogue with God, an encounter combining utter surrender with fierce demands.

Practically everything in the life of St. Catherine was incredible. In our days of dwindling family size, even her birth was remarkable as the twenty-fourth child of a twin birth! The other baby died immediately. Her mother was so saddened by this loss that she hastened to ensure a replacement, bringing the family size to twenty-five children!

As a little girl, Catherine was lively, stubborn, and direct. Unlike many of the saints, she was never considered beautiful. Her adoring biographer and spiritual son, Blessed Raymond of Capua, says that she was never anything much to look at. Later on when Catherine ate nothing but the Holy Eucharist, she appeared to be like "a bag of bones." Nonetheless, the child was so charming that everyone loved her very much.

At the age of six Catherine was gifted with a miraculous grace that would shape the rest of her life. She had been running an errand and paused for a moment to look across the valley. In the sky she suddenly saw a vision of heaven, the Savior with Peter, Paul, and John the Evangelist. The Lord smiled on her with great love and made the sign of the cross over her head.

This and subsequent visions led her to want to devote herself to God as a virgin. When her parents tried to marry her off—hoping to reap financial benefits from a good match—Catherine cut off her hair! To show the recalcitrant maiden the advantages of being married, her parents decided to punish her by making her do all the servile work in the house. This only inspired Catherine to make a cell of her own heart and to render menial service with such zeal that all were amazed.

When her own father saw a vision of Jesus talking to his daughter, he became ashamed of his ambitious plans. He commented that he doubted if he could really find a match more wonderful than Christ himself.

Then followed a three-year period of solitude where Catherine was allowed to stay in her little room, while the household bustled around her. But at the age of twenty-one, Jesus told her that he wanted to send her out into the world to save souls. To facilitate his plan, Jesus personally taught her how to read, using the breviary as his textbook.

By this time Catherine was also less and less able to eat and lived mostly on the Holy Eucharist. Her union with the Lord was sealed by an experience of mystical marriage.

Catherine's outside activities initially involved ministering to the sick and the destitute. Her biographer, who knew her personally, actually added up the weight of huge quantities of produce that this saint took from the family larder and brought in the middle of the night tied around her waist to the home of a starving family miles away.

On another occasion Catherine persuaded a political prisoner to return to the sacraments before his death, with a promise to come to the guillotine with him and provide comfort when the ax would fall. Catherine kept her promise. Holding his severed head in her hands, she meditated long on the blood of the prisoner and the redeeming blood of the Savior. Afterwards in a vision she saw the soul of the young man entering the wounded side of Christ.

Gradually a "family" of priests and lay people began to surround the saint. Catherine would read hearts and bring sinners to want to confess and receive absolution. When she became a Third Order Dominican she came under the direction of Raymond of Capua. This led to the spread of her activities into the realm of church politics—during the time of disputes about the papacy. Catherine wrote to the pope demanding his return to Rome and even traveled to Avignon to plead with him. During such trips she began to preach openly to the people with great fire.

We should not imagine that everyone drank in her words with loving obedience. Many even mocked her openly. By the end of her life the saint was filled with a sense of failure at all her initiatives toward church reform.

In 1377 Catherine began to dictate the locutions the Lord sent to her in astounding profusion. The book taken down by several priest-secretaries is called *The Dialogue.* So many important theological topics are treated in this book that it would be impossible to do justice to them in a summary. I would suggest that readers take the trouble to study it themselves. *The Dialogue* is a classic of spirituality as important and influential as the major books of other Doctors of the Church.

In 1378 Catherine went to Rome with an entourage of some twenty-four disciples in an effort to urge Pope Urban to resolve the papal schism. When the group ran out of food, Catherine herself would go out to beg. She spent most of her time at St. Peter's Church praying for unity and reform and speaking to the pope and to the cardinals. This saint's teaching on overcoming difficulties in the church sounds most modern indeed: "Not by... violence will [the Church] regain her beauty but through peace and through the constant humble prayers and sweat and tears poured out by my servants with eager desire."[3]

One of the most popular of all prophetic holy women, St. Catherine died in 1380 in Rome. What is her central message? The latest translator of *The Dialogue*, Suzanne Noffke, O.P., writes in her introduction that while some say it was Truth, "others contend it was Love. Both are in fact right. For Catherine God is 'gentle first Truth' and God is made with love and charity itself. The way to God is the constantly lived dynamic of knowledge and love."[4]

Noffke adds that Catherine was also "a social mystic—but even more properly a mystic activist. Poverty, sickness, the suffering of injustice even to the point of death, were not merely evils or even systemic evils to her: they were that, and as such she fought them—but they were still more pawns in the hand of the will of *both* oppressed and oppressor under God.... If she would be used and abused and to all appearances fail, she would pay that price."[5]

As concerns the intimate side of her teaching, the most famous passage is a word from God to Catherine: "Do you know, daughter, who you are and who I am? If you know these two things you have beatitude in your grasp. You are she who is not, and I AM WHO IS. Let your soul but become penetrated with this truth, and the Enemy can never lead you astray; you will never be caught in any snare of his, nor ever transgress any commandment of mine; you will have set your feet on the royal road which leads to the fulness of grace, and truth, and light."[6]

Total humility is the hallmark of Catherine's spirituality. Even the devil commends her for it: "Damnable woman! There is no getting at you! If I throw you down in confusion you lift yourself up to mercy. If I exalt you you throw yourself down. You come even to hell in your humility, and even in hell you hound me. So I will not come back to you again, because you beat me with the cudgel of charity!"[7]

Along with humility came a burning desire for the salvation not only of herself but of all mankind. Within her own body Catherine would long for the Bread of Life and beg Blessed Raymond, her confessor and companion, to avoid delay in saying Mass so that she might receive as soon as possible. God told her the Eucharist "is the food of angels and the food of life. It is a food that satisfies the hungry soul who finds joy in this bread, but not those who are not hungry, for it is a good that must be taken with the mouth of holy desire and tasted in love. So you see how I have provided for your strengthening."[8]

Even a nodding acquaintance with the life and words of St. Catherine of Siena can leave us in a state of awe and wonder. If her spirituality is normal, we are less than underachievers! Yet each of us is called to be the best version of ourselves, just as Catherine grew to such tremendous stature by means of her complete surrender to the Master Creator. Let us never tire of giving ourselves trustfully to God to make of us what he will.

MERCY

The mercy of God is the most prevalent theme in the writings of St. Catherine. Throughout Christ's prophetic words in The Dialogue, *we are shown the pain of the Savior at the rejection of his mercy by the indifferent and the sinful. In the light of the merciful love of Christ for us, we are enjoined to also display compassion for those who most upset or persecute us.*

O eternal Mercy, you who cover over your creatures' faults!... By your mercy we were created. And by your mercy we were created anew in your Son's blood. It is your mercy that preserves us. Your mercy made your Son play death against life and life against death on the wood of the cross. In him life confounded the death that is our sin, even while that same death of sin robbed the spotless Lamb of his bodily life. But who was conquered? Death! And how? By your mercy!... O mad lover! It was not enough for you to take on our humanity: You had to die as well! Nor was death enough: You descended to the depths to summon our holy ancestors and fulfill your truth and mercy in them. Your goodness promises good to those who serve you in truth, so you went to call these servants of yours from their suffering to reward them for their labors! I see your mercy pressing you to give us even more when you leave yourself with us as food to strengthen our weakness, so that we forgetful fools should be forever reminded of your goodness. Every day you give us this food, showing us yourself in the sacrament of the altar within the mystic body of holy Church. And what has done this? Your mercy."[9]

In answer to Catherine's petition to learn more about how to judge the virtue and vice of others, Jesus describes the attitude of the true Christian soul as it nears death: "She does not turn back to look at her past virtues because she does not want to place her trust in them but only in the blood wherein my mercy is to be found. And just as she lived mindful of the blood, so in death she is immersed and inebriated in the blood. The devils cannot reproach her for sin because in her lifetime she conquered their malice with wisdom, and now they come around to see whether they can still make some small gain. So they come in horrible forms to frighten her with their hideously foul appearance and with all sorts of fantasies. But because there is none of sin's venom in the soul, their appearance does not frighten her as it would someone else who had lived sinfully in the world.

"When the devils see that the soul has entered into the blood ablaze with charity, they cannot bear it, but from far off they keep shooting their arrows. But their fighting and screaming does no harm to that soul, for she has already begun to taste eternal life. Her mind's eye with its pupil of most holy faith sees me, her infinite eternal reward whom she is waiting to possess—not because she deserves it but as a gift of my grace in the blood of Christ my Son. So she stretches out her arms of hope and reaches out for it with the hands of love, entering into possession even before she is actually there. And as soon as she has passed through the narrow gate of the Word, immersed in his blood, she comes to me, the sea of peace."[10]

Concerning the merciful attitude of Christians toward others, God tells Catherine: "They find joy in everything. They do not sit in judgment on my servants or anyone else, but rejoice in every situation and every way of living they see, saying, 'Thanks to you, eternal Father, that in your house there are so many dwelling places!' And they are happier to see many different ways than if they were to see everyone walking the same way, because this way they see the greatness of my goodness more fully revealed. In everything they find joy and the fragrance of the rose. This is true not only of good things; even when they see something that is clearly sinful they do not pass judgment, but rather feel a holy and genuine compassion, praying for the sinner and saying with perfect humility, 'Today it is your turn; tomorrow it will be mine unless divine grace holds me up.'"[11]

THE PURIFICATION OF THE CHURCH

I find it difficult to think of any mystic who had a greater love than Catherine for the mystical Body of Christ in the throes of its sinfulness.

My Lord, turn the eye of your mercy on your people and on your mystic body, holy Church.... For what would it mean to me to have eternal life if death were the lot of your people, or if my faults especially and those of your other creatures should bring darkness upon your bride, who is light itself? It is my will, then, and I beg it as a favor, that you have mercy on your people with the same eternal love that led you to create us in your image and likeness.[12]

In answer to Catherine's desire to know how we should react to the evils in the church, God says: "You ought to despise and hate the ministers' sins, and try to dress them in the new clothes of charity and holy prayer, and wash away their filth with your tears. In other words, you should hold them out to me with tears and great desire, so that I in my goodness may clothe them with the garment of charity.... For it is not my will that they should administer the Sun to you out of their darksomeness…. Indeed, I have appointed them and given them to you to be angels on earth and suns, as I have told you. When they are less than that, you ought to pray for them. But you are not to judge them. Leave the judging to me, and I, because of your prayers and my own desire, will be merciful to them. If they will not change their ways, the dignity they have will be their destruction. And if the great reproof they receive from me, the supreme Judge, at the moment of death does not make them change or reach out for my generous mercy, they will be condemned to eternal fire."[13]

"My daughter, let your respite be in glorifying and praising my name, in offering me the incense of constant prayer for these poor wretches who have sunk so low and made themselves deserving of divine judgment for their sins. And let your place of refuge be my only-begotten Son, Christ crucified. Make your home and hiding place in the cavern of his open side…. Once you see and taste this love you will follow his teaching and find your nourishment at the table of the cross. In other words, charity will make you put up with your neighbors with true patience by enduring pain, torment, and weariness no matter what their source. In this way you will flee and escape the leprosy."[14]

You would have me know myself and your goodness, and the sins committed against you by every class of people and especially by your ministers, so that I might draw tears from the knowledge of your infinite goodness and let them flow as a river over my wretched self and over these wretched living dead. Therefore it is my will, ineffable Fire, joyous Love, eternal Father, that my desire should never weary of longing for your honor and the salvation of souls.... Let my eyes never rest, but in your grace make of them two rivers for the water that flows from you, the sea of peace. Thank you, thank you, Father![15]

RESPONDING TO GOD'S BURNING LOVE

The lines of St. Catherine about the love of God are so passionate that we wonder at our own lack of focus. May we allow them to enkindle us with the same kind of fervor.

O immeasurably tender love! Who would not be set afire with such love? What heart could keep from breaking? You, deep well of charity, it seems you are so madly in love with your creatures that you could not live without us! Yet you are our God, and have no need of us. Your greatness is no greater for our well-being, nor are you harmed by any harm that comes to us, for you are supreme eternal Goodness. What could move you to such mercy? Neither duty nor any need you have of us (we are sinful and wicked debtors!)—but only love![16]

O eternal God, light surpassing all other light because all light comes forth from you! O fire surpassing every fire because you alone are the fire that burns without consuming! You consume whatever sin and selfishness you find in the soul. Yet your consuming does not distress the soul but fattens her with insatiable love, for though you satisfy her she is never sated but longs for you constantly. The more she desires you the more she finds and enjoys you, high eternal fire, abyss of charity![17]

O eternal Father! O fiery abyss of charity!... Why then are you so mad? Because you have fallen in love with what you have made! You are pleased and delighted over her within yourself, as if you were drunk with desire for her salvation. She runs away from you and you go looking for her. She strays and you draw closer to her. You clothed yourself in our humanity and nearer than that you could not have come. And what shall I say? I will stutter, "A-a," because there is nothing else I know how to say. Finite language cannot express the emotion of the soul who longs for you infinitely.... I have nothing to add from these clumsy emotions of mine. I say only, my soul, that you have tasted and seen the abyss of supreme eternal providence.[18]

O eternal Trinity, fire and abyss of charity, dissolve this very day the cloud of my body! I am driven to desire, in the knowledge of yourself that you have given me in your truth, to leave behind the weight of this body of mine and give my life for the glory and praise of your name. For by the light of understanding... I have tasted and seen your depth, eternal Trinity, and the beauty of your creation.... O abyss! O eternal Godhead! O deep sea! What more could you have given me than the gift of your very self?... You are a fire lifting all chill and giving light. In your light you have made me know your truth.... Good above every good, joyous Good, Good beyond measure and understanding! Beauty above all beauty.... You who are the angels' good are given to humans with burning love. You, garment who covers all nakedness, pasture the starving within your sweetness, for you are sweet without trace of bitterness.[19]

8

Saint Joan of Arc
(1412–1431)

Alas that I should be treated so horribly and cruelly that my entire body, which has never known impurity, should today be consumed and reduced to ashes. I would rather be decapitated seven times over than be thus burned. Before God, the great judge, I appeal against the great wrongs and injustices done to me.[1]

✠ ✠ ✠

ST. JOAN OF ARC has been universally lauded as an example of courage in the face of impossible odds. Even the skeptical and cynical Mark Twain considered her to be the only good person ever to have lived on this earth. This atheist devoted twelve years to research his recently reprinted biography.[2]

The inclusion of this famous saint in a book of prayers of the mystics poses interesting challenges. Since we have very few long vocal prayers of St. Joan in writing and also have no record of her having ascended the usual stages of mystical prayer, there might seem to be reason to omit Joan from this anthology.

Nonetheless, Joan's mystical graces have had perhaps the greatest influence on history of anyone. Some might question if perhaps all of France would have become a colony of England were it not for this simple country girl.[3] She turned the tide of history by obeying the heavenly voices which commanded her to crown the lawful French king and later to lead the defense of her country against the English enemy. Aside from the saints described in Scripture, St. Joan of Arc perhaps shares with St. Francis of Assisi the distinction of being the most well-known and beloved by non-Christians.

Joan of Arc was born in a tumultuous period of French history when the evils of war were compounded by doubt of lawful succession to the crown. Here is the charming description of her youth given by another great admirer, Hilaire Belloc:

> She grew up tall and sturdy, strong of body and clear of mind, and vigorous at her tasks of spinning and all housework; she would tend sheep and she would plough upon their half-hundred acres, for her father was a yeoman. Also she was famous at her needle. As a child she played round the fairies' beech tree in the place, hanging garlands, singing and dancing there, she and her three brothers and her little sister Catherine and the other children of the hamlet; and at home her mother taught her the Hail Mary and the Our Father and the Creed. It was in a pleasant

valley with long hills on either side and woods upon them, and the young River Meuse flowed by.

One summer morning, when she was thirteen years of age and some months more, she went into the meadows to gather flowers…. A dazzling light shone by her at her right hand, supplanting the day, and she was overcome with terror; till, from the midst of the glory, came a voice which spoke of the faith and its observance, and at last gave order that she should seek the uncrowned King of France, dispossessed by his foes, and rescue him and crown him at Rheims. At the third summons she saw St. Michael in his splendor and about him the soldiery of Heaven.[4]

We all know the rest, or do we? I always knew that Joan adopted male dress, but I didn't know that this disguise was not so much to gain acceptance by the other soldiers as to protect herself from rape! I always knew that Joan surprised the court when she was able to identify the disguised Dauphin, Charles VII. What I did not know was that she was able to do so by means of infused insight. I knew that Joan valiantly led the soldiers who had come to admire her greatly, but I didn't know that her standard bore the words "Jesus, Maria."

I always knew that Joan was finally captured, betrayed by the French allies of the English, tortured, and condemned in a trumped-up ecclesiastical trial. I did not know that she had briefly succumbed and recanted out of terror of death by fire, but that Joan repented and was dragged to the stake to be burned to death. This young woman's last moments were full of pleading prayers for the strength she did not have of her own nature.

The knowledge that this great saint suffered a most understandable time of weakness gives me courage. Holiness does not consist in never falling, but in reaching up from the pit to let the waiting hand of God bring us back to our feet.

Some love the image of Joan because they think of her as a rebel who set her own intuitions against the authority of the church. While she did try to avoid unjust punishment at the hands of the local hierarchy, which was actually in league with the enemy, Joan was eager to have her case decided by the pope. When asked by her persecutors if she was certain she was in God's grace, Joan replied with humble candor: "If I am not, may God put me there; and if I am, may God so keep me. I should be the saddest creature in the world if I knew I were not in His grace."[5]

I want to conclude this brief biographical summary with the reflections of my co-author of *Great Saints, Great Friends,* Sister Mary Neill, O.P. I will never forget the wracking sobs that came from her room in the convent as she researched the life of St. Joan. She wrote:

> l feel such enormous passion and pain as I read the trial and death of Joan that I know it is related to games I've played in my life, games I've been caught in. But centrally, my passion for Joan pon-

ders the generosity demanded by God, by life, by Christ in order to live from authentic being, to have an authentic voice, to follow your inner voice.... My body and soul protest as I read Joan's story. Sometimes the price seems too dear. It seems to me too dear as an onlooker. But if Joan, who never lied, said that God would be with her in that great final payment, I trust that He was— no, I trust her trust of Him. She knew Him well because she obeyed Him and was comforted by Him and His friends.... Why don't more of us become friends of God, become saints, receive His crown and His comfort? To do so is to endanger our power in the world's games (the games grow tiresome, but we know them well) and we are addicted to looking good and feeling good rather than to being good."[6]

THE PRAYERS OF ST. JOAN OF ARC

The prayers of St. Joan do not fit into three or four categories, but are best excerpted in a historical sequence based on her witness during her trial. She herself insisted that some revelations not be made known publicly since they were for the king instead of the judges. We are also able to draw upon the reports of the many friends and on-lookers who stood in awe of her passionate missionary zeal.

Asked what the voice told her at the beginning of her supposed call: It told her to be good and to go to church often; and that she must come to France [in those days not all of what we now call France was so called]... that she should raise the siege of the city of Orléans... that she, Jeanne, [Joan] should go to Robert de Baudricourt, in the town of Vaucouleurs of which he was captain, and he would provide an escort for her.... When she reached Vaucouleurs she easily recognized Robert de Baudricourt, although she had never seen him before; and she knew him through her voice, for the voice had told her it was he....[7]

Subsequently she heard many voices about the Duke of Orléans and also about the king, whom she first saw at the castle of Chinon: She recognized him among many others by the counsel of her voice, which revealed him to her.... Her voice had promised her that as soon as she should come to the king he would receive her. She said also that those of her party knew well that the voice was sent to Jeanne from God, and they knew this voice. She said further that her king and several others heard the voices which came to the said Jeanne.... Then Jeanne said that there is not a day when she does not hear this voice; and she has much need of it. She said she never asked of it any final reward but the salvation of her soul....[8]

At this point in the trial they asked her whether she was still hearing voices, even that very day: She answered: "I heard it yesterday and today... once in the morning, once at vespers, and once when the Ave Maria was rung in the evening...." She asked counsel of it.

Whereupon the voice told her to answer boldly [the questions at the trial] and God would comfort her.[9]

Asked whether the voice was always from an angel or from saints or straight from God, Joan replied: "The voice was of St. Catherine and of St. Margaret. And their heads were crowned in a rich and precious fashion with beautiful crowns."... She knew one from the other by the greeting they gave her.... "I saw them with my bodily eyes as well as I see you; and when they left me, I wept; and I fain would have had them take me with them too."... She would rather be torn asunder by horses than have come to France without God's leave.[10]

"Everything I have done is at God's command; and if He had ordered me to assume a different habit [than the male attire she wore] I should have done it."... Asked whether she calls St. Catherine or St. Margaret or whether they come without being called, she answered: "They often come without my calling," and sometimes if they did not come, she would pray God to send them.[11]

Asked whether she did reverence to St. Michael and the angels, when she saw them, she answered that she did, and kissed the ground where they had stood after they had gone. Asked whether the said angels were long with her, she answered that they often came among the Christian folk and were not seen, and she often saw them amongst the Christian folk.

... [The voices addressed her as] Jeanne the Maid, daughter of God.[12]

Joan proclaimed that it was an angel who brought the king his crown: "When the angel came before the king, he did the king reverence by bowing before him and pronouncing the words of the sign.... And with this the angel recalled to the king the sweet patience he had shown in the many great tribulations which had befallen him.... Many churchmen saw the crown who did not see the angel.... It was brought from God, and no goldsmith on earth could have made one so rich and fair....[13]

Once she jumped from a tower rather than be taken captive by the English: Asked whether the leap was made at the counsel of her voices, she answered that St. Catherine told her almost every day not to jump, and God would help her...."You must be resigned and not falter; you will not be delivered until you have seen the King of the English." Jeanne answered: "Truly I do not want to see him, and I would rather die than fall into the hands of the English."... After falling from the tower, for two or three days she was without food and so injured by the leap that she could not eat or drink; yet she was comforted by St. Catherine who told her to confess and ask God to forgive her for having jumped out.... Asked whether when she leapt she expected to kill herself, she answered no, for as she leaped she commended herself to God. And she hoped that by the leap she would escape and not be delivered to the English.[14]

Asked whether, since her voices had told her that in the end she should go to Paradise, she has felt assured of her salvation, and of not being damned in hell, she answered that she firmly believed what the voices told her, namely that she will be saved, as firmly as if she were already there.[15]

After being condemned by the judges and tortured: She asked her voices if she would be burned and they answered that she must wait upon God, and He would aid her.[16]

The first time she is brought to the stake, Joan recanted out of terror at the fire. Afterwards in prison, Joan is asked about her state of mind since her recantation: God had sent her word through St. Catherine and St. Margaret of the great pity of this treason by which she consented to abjure and recant in order to save her life; that she had damned herself to save her life....[17]

On the day on which she was condemned... the body of Jesus Christ was brought to her.... Friar Martin heard her confession.... Then she was led to the Vieux Marché, and beside her walked Friar Martin and myself [a priest], with an escort of eight hundred soldiers armed with axes and swords.... She uttered pious and devout lamentations and called on the blessed Trinity, and on the blessed and glorious Virgin Mary, and on all the blessed Saints in Paradise, naming many of them in her devotion and her true confession of faith.... The judges who were present and even several of the English were

moved to great tears and weeping. She asked most
fervently to be given a cross. And when an English-
man who was present heard this he made her one
out of wood from the end of a stick and handed it to
her. She received it and kissed it most devotedly,
uttering pious lamentations and acknowledging
God our Redeemer, who suffered for our redemption on the Cross.... Then she put that Cross on her
breast between her body and her clothes, and
humbly asked me to let her have the Crucifix from
the church so that she could gaze on it continuously
until her death.... And her last word, as she died,
was a loud cry of "Jesus."[18]

*These final lines from the proceedings of the retrial witness
to the holiness of this great prophetic mystic:* One of the
English, a soldier who particularly loathed Joan...
[saw] a white dove flying from the direction of
France at the moment when she was giving up the
ghost. And the executioner, after his midday meal on
that same day, came to the Dominican convent and
said to me that he greatly feared he was damned, for
he had burnt a saint.[19]

9

Saint Catherine of Genoa
(1447–1510)

O Love, who shall impede me from loving you? Though I were not only in the world as I am, but in a camp of soldiers, I could not be impeded from loving you.[1]

✠ ✠ ✠

BORN IN GENOA TO A NOBLE FAMILY, Catherine was surrounded by luxuries. But at the age of eight, the little girl began to practice penance by sleeping at night on straw instead of in her own bed. She was a quiet and obedient child, gifted with so many graces that by the age of thirteen she was pleading with her parents to let her enter a convent.

By sixteen, however, she reluctantly agreed to marry Giuliano Adorno, a man from a similar background but of quite a different temperament. In fact her husband was peevish and imprudent to the point of bankrupting the family. In the 1551 biography called *The Book of the Admirable Life and Holy Doctrine of the Blessed Caterinetta of Genoa*, we read that "in order to prevent her from setting her love on the world and the flesh, God permitted that she should be given a husband whose character was the very opposite of her own."[2]

During the first ten years of their marriage, Catherine sought refuge in feminine company. In retrospect, she thought her behavior during this sad time had been frivolous and did many penances for her offenses against God. No amount of diversion, however, could overcome the deep melancholy arising from the incompatibilities that persisted between Catherine and her husband.

Such a story is surely not uncommon in the history of marriage. What is remarkable is the conversion which changed Catherine's whole way of life. Urged on by one of her sisters who was a nun, Catherine agreed to go to the confessional of a holy priest.

She had hardly knelt down... when her heart was suddenly pierced by an immense love of God, with such a clear awareness of her own miseries and sins and of God's goodness, that she was ready to swoon. The feeling produced in her a change of heart that purified her and drew her wholly away from the follies of the world.... She cried out in her heart with burning love: "No more world! No more sin!"

... While she thus knelt, incapable of speech and almost senseless, her confessor did not notice anything amiss. He was called away on some matter, and when he returned shortly afterwards, she recovered.... Rising to her feet, she left him and returned home, all on fire.... As if beside herself, she chose out the most private room there was, and there gave vent to her burning tears and sighs. The only prayer she could think of to say was: "O Love, is it possible that you have called me with so much love and have revealed to me in one moment what no tongue can describe?"

In the following days the only sounds that came from her were deep sighs, and so keen was the sorrow she felt for the sins she had committed against God's goodness that if she had not been sustained by a superhuman power, her heart would have burst and she would have surely died. Christ appeared to her in spirit with His Cross on His shoulder, dripping with blood. The whole house seemed to her to be full of streams of blood, and she saw that it had all been shed for love alone. Horror of sin and disgust at herself made her cry out: "O Lord, if it is necessary, I am ready to confess my sins in public."[3]

After this experience, Catherine would often see the bleeding Sacred Heart of the Savior on the cross suffering for love of us sinners. While still attending to her domestic duties, she managed to spend six hours a day in prayer—often so rapt in divine love that she could not see or hear anything going on around her. So much did Catherine love Holy Communion that she would suffer bodily pain if deprived of it for even one day. When she saw the host in the priest's hands, she would say within herself: "Now quickly, quickly, send it down to my heart, for it is the food of it."[4]

Throughout her life, Catherine devoted herself to the poor and especially to the sick, often handling the most disgusting objects in the process of cleaning. She would kiss the most incurable, risking infection to herself. God's grace protected her from any harmful consequences of these deeds of love.

Since Catherine's way of life was so radically different from that of her husband, he finally agreed to live with her as brother and sister and allowed her enough solitude to follow the Lord in the ways he was leading her. Eventually, Giuliano became a Third Order Franciscan and died a holy death.

Catherine's contemplative life was certainly not one mostly of delight. The accounts of her inward trials are terrifying. Her biographer describes some of them:

> She would bite her hands and burn them, and this in order to divert, if possible, her interior oppression.... The only person left with whom she found any relief was her confessor, but then he too was taken away from her, and it came to the point that there was nothing more he could say to her or do to help her. At times she would seem to have her mind in a mill and it were grinding her, soul and body. Then she would... retire alone into a room and throw herself on the ground crying, "Love, I cannot bear it any longer!" She would continue with great lamentation, writhing like a serpent, and her moans could be heard by all those in the house.[5]

Catherine suffered most from extreme loneliness, so different was she from those around her. Finding it more and more unbearable to keep living after having seen something of the joys of eternal life, she would pray: "O Lord, what would you have me do further in this world? I neither see nor hear, nor eat nor sleep. I do not know what I do or what I say. I feel as though I were a dead thing. There is no creature that understands me. I find myself lonely, unknown, poor, naked, strange and different from the rest of the world."[6]

When the time of her death finally drew near, Catherine experienced a joy so great that she was convulsed with laughter. "She was quite light-hearted and showed it by peals of merry laughter. When asked the cause, she said she had seen some most beautiful, merry and joyous faces, so that she could not refrain from laughing."[7] Her happiness was followed by great physical pain, but after several weeks of agony she died with these words on her lips: "Love of God... Sweetness of God... Charity, union, and peace.... God, God."[8]

The teachings of St. Catherine of Genoa are admired for their fresh, striking qualities, so different from textbook theological formulations. Her most famous saying is: "God is my being, my me, my strength, my happiness, my good, my delight.... I will have nothing to do with a love that would be *for* God or *in* God. I cannot bear the word *for* or the word *in*, because they denote something that may be in between God and me. This is the love that pure love cannot bear since pure love is God Himself."[9]

Here is another example of her unconventional way of describing classical spiritual truths:

> Take some bread and eat it. When you have eaten it, its substance goes to nourish the body, and the remainder, the superfluous part, is evacuated, because nature has no use for it, and indeed, if it were to retain it, the body would die. Now, if the bread were to say to you: "Why do you take my being from me? It is not in my nature to like being annihilated. If I could, I would defend myself from you in order to save myself, an action natural to every creature." You would answer: "Bread, your being was meant for the sustenance of my body, which is of more worth than you, and so you ought to be more content with the end for which you were created than with simply being. It is only your end that makes your being of any value; it gives you your dignity, which you cannot attain except by means of your annihilation.... This is what God does [by means of death] with man who is created for eternal life as his end.[10]

I would not be surprised if St. Catherine of Genoa was one of the mystics described in this book whom you would least like to imitate. It would be easy to dismiss her as a demented woman. In fact, many who knew her when she lived held such an opinion of her. Perhaps you might be happy to think that God has a way not only of saving but even of sanctifying personality types quite different from your own.

Yet, even if I don't identify with Catherine perfectly, I find that if I allow her words to bury themselves in my heart, slowly I hear an echo. And, with that sense of kinship—in spite of all differences—comes comfort. No excess is so great that it cannot be encompassed by the love that evoked it, when that love is divine.

DESIRE FOR COMPLETE UNION WITH GOD

All of the mystics claim that union with God exceeds the joys of all other unions. Let us see how St. Catherine of Genoa leads us to this truth.

O tender Love, I want all of you. I could not live if I thought I were to do without even a spark of you.[11]

Her Love once said within her mind: "In Holy Scripture take Love, with which you will ever go straightly, exactly, lightly, attentively, swiftly, without error, without guide, and without the means of other creatures, since love is sufficient for itself to do all things without fear or weariness, so that martyrdom itself appears a joy."[12]

God said to her interiorly: "I do not wish you henceforward to turn your eyes except toward Love. Here I want you to stay and not to move, whatever happens to you or to others, within or without, make up your mind to be as if dead to all else, for whoever has trust in me ought not to doubt about himself."[13] While I live I shall always say to the world: "Do with me what you will on the outside, but inside let me be, for I cannot be occupied inside with anything else but God. He has taken hold of me inside, and locked me inside Himself so firmly that He will be open to anyone!"[14]

O my God, all mine, everything is mine, because all that belongs to God seems all to belong to me.[15]

WISHING TO DO GOD'S WILL

Many Christians are ready for remarkable sacrifices out of love of God and neighbor, but only on their own terms. "His will is our peace," wrote Dante. Whenever we cannot understand God's will in the happenings in our lives, we need to pray for trust.

O Love, if others feel an obligation to observe your commandments, I freely will to have them all ten, because they are all delightful and full of love. You do not command things that do harm, but to those who observe them, you give great peace, love and union with yourself.... For though the divine precepts are contrary to our sensuality, yet they are in accord with the spirit. The spirit by its nature is ever longing to be free from all bodily sensations, so as to be able to unite itself to God through love.[16]

Her Love once said within her mind: "Observe these three rules. Never say 'I will,' or 'I will not.' Never say 'my' but always 'our.'"[17]

O Love, with what tender deceit you deceived me,

to steal all my self-love from me and clothe me in pure love, full of all joys.[18]

You are my understanding, and I shall know what it shall please you I should know. I shall not weary myself with further seeking, but I will abide in peace with your understanding, which holds possession of my mind.[19]

LONGING FOR PURITY OF HEART

Such close union with God could not be without anguish because of the many imperfections of even a holy soul. But why should someone see seemingly small defects as offenses against God in the first place? We find a clue in our human loves. Don't we feel worse when we display a weakness in front of someone we especially admire? How much more if the beloved one is hoping that his or her love would heal us of the insecurities revealed in sin. The offense comes when our behavior manifests the fact that some trifle is worth more to us than even love. Such defects include not only addictions of the flesh but also those virtues which themselves can become vices if worn with pride.

My Love, I can bear anything else, but to have offended you is too horrible and unbearable. Give me any other penance, but not that of seeing I have offended you. I do not wish to have committed the offenses I have committed against you. I cannot consent to have ever offended you. At the hour of death show me rather the devils with all their terrors and torments. I consider them as nothing in comparison with the sight of the least offense against you.[20]

When my self found it was discovered and could not deny these imperfections uncovered by Love, it turned to Him and said: "Since your eye is so sharp and penetrating, I give you welcome. Keep on with what you are doing, though I feel the pain of it. Content your will, strip me of this unsightly covering and clothe me with Love, full, pure, and sincere.[21]

Love annihilated not only the outer malignant part of me, but also the inner spiritual part.... [Love said,] "I want you all for myself. Do not think I shall spare you the smallest possession of soul or body. I will leave you stark naked. I am so keen-eyed that, when I begin to sift you, every perfection remains a defect in my sight. The higher up you may go, however great a perfection you may have, the higher will I ever stand above you, to ruin all your perfections."[22]

YEARNING FOR ETERNAL LIFE

A love of God as intense as that of St. Catherine cannot but long for the fruition of eternal union.

Once hearing a preacher say: "Arise, O dead, and come to judgement," she shouted loudly in an excess of love, "I want to come now, now!" and all who heard her were astonished.[23]

I find only one fault with you, death, that you are too niggardly with those who long for you, and too lavish with those who flee from you.[24]

10

Saint Teresa of Avila
(1515–1582)

Let nothing disturb thee,
Let nothing dismay thee.
All things pass.
God never changes.
Patience attains
all that it strives for.
He who has God
finds he lacks nothing.
God alone suffices.[1]

✠ ✠ ✠

WITH ST. CATHERINE OF SIENA, Teresa of Avila is one of the two women mystics who have been proclaimed Doctors of the Church.[2] The writings of this famous Carmelite nun are among the most seminal and popular—in spite of the fact that she was not a highly educated woman.

Teresa's chatty, humorous, and natural style draws the reader into her stories. Teachings that can be daunting when presented in the style of her great mentor John of the Cross become readily available. This is true not only of her autobiography but also of more structured works such as *The Interior Castle.*

Teresa was the third daughter of a large upper-class Spanish family. She showed spurts of piety but was also rather wild. Probably because of her flirtatious tendencies, she was sent away to a convent school after the death of her mother. In fact, this vivacious, charming, young woman was not at all inclined to religious life. But she thought it at least better than being a wife and mother, so burdensome did those duties appear from watching the miseries of her own mother.

Once professed as a nun, Teresa began a long "double life." She enjoyed talking for hours with the guests in the parlour. Meanwhile, the Lord himself was leading her into deep contemplative prayer. Twenty years of visions, locutions, and raptures were necessary before Teresa was willing to break with her desire for constant human fellowship and actively seek greater seclusion.

Most of the convents and monasteries in her day were quite worldly—largely because anyone who didn't want to marry was sent to religious establishments even if they had no real vocation. Numerous visions and locutions convinced Teresa that God wanted her to found reformed Carmelite convents and monasteries which would foster true prayer.

St. John of the Cross was seeking the same kind of purity of soul. With his help, Teresa began to found small religious houses throughout Spain. Her work entailed all sorts of vexatious journeys and business transactions, under the direction of the Lord himself—who appeared to Teresa as often as he had to Catherine of Siena.

Anyone who reads Teresa's writings will soon realize that seclusion did not mean a hermit-like existence. Even though her new reformed life brought with it much more time for prayer, she also enjoyed plenty of opportunity for ministry. Large numbers of people were attracted to Teresa's lively personality as well as her holiness.

Quite obviously the attraction was mutual, as Teresa writes in her autobiography:

> I had a serious fault, which led me into great trouble. It was that if I began to realize that a person liked me, and I took to him myself, I would grow so fond of him that my memory would feel compelled to revert to him and I would always be thinking of him, without intentionally giving any offence to God.... This was such a harmful thing that it was ruining my soul. But when once I had seen the great beauty of the Lord [in a vision] I saw no one who by comparison with Him seemed acceptable to me on whom my thoughts wished to dwell.... And, unless for my sins the Lord allows this memory to fade, I consider it impossible for me to be so deeply absorbed in anything that I do not regain my freedom when I turn once more in thought, even for a moment, to this Lord.[3]

Teresa did her writing, under obedience, at odd moments between prayer, travel, and needlework. The teaching that has been the most helpful to others is the description of the stages of prayer in *The Interior Castle*. A brief explanation of the image of the castle may give readers unfamiliar with the book a framework for understanding the prayers in this spiritual classic.

Teresa saw in a vision a clear crystal castle composed of many rooms or mansions. The first mansions contain people who have given up the sins of the world. Their prayer is mostly intercessory, begging God to free the soul from its attachments to the sins it enjoyed before seeking a closer union with God. In the second mansions, believers are led to seek the company of the good, to receive the sacraments often, and to pray with much warmth and light. In the third mansions, we find the highly virtuous Christians who are still not totally surrendered to God. They are often self-righteous. Although they occasionally catch glimpses of the King, their prayer is frequently dry.

Teresa suggests that those who want to advance beyond the third mansions must come under good spiritual direction. They must obey this director and absolutely avoid fault-finding, replacing this with silence. The fourth mansions open to such a seeker, with grace flowing more freely. Teresa compares this flow to the difference between laboriously drawing water out of a well and obtaining it by means of a water-wheel.

Dwellers of the fifth mansions of the interior castle experience spiritual trances and great joy, but also grief about the state of the world. The sixth mansions are like an engagement period for those hoping to be married in the future. Here we find raptures, locutions, interior visions, and even levitations. Dreadful crosses also assault the believer in the form of ridicule, persecution, fear of self-deceit, and desire for the fruition of union that cannot be achieved on this earth.

Only in the seventh mansions do we come to complete union in the spiritual marriage. God and the soul become as inseparable as rain is from a river into which it falls. Effects of spiritual marriage are self-forgetfulness, desire to suffer for the kingdom, joy in the midst of persecution, immediate forgiveness of enemies, and great fervor in helping others.

Teresa herself is surely an example of a soul living in the seventh mansions. Her love of Christ as her Spouse was ecstatic. She was always cheerful yet also suffered from many extremely unpleasant maladies, including migraine headaches. Teresa died in 1582 after one of the longest and most fruitful lives in the history of spirituality. The prayers I have chosen are from *Exclamations of the Soul to God.*[4]

Many times we develop a fixed image of what is a "holy woman." Often our mental ideal is one who is totally self-contained, noble, without any visible flaws. We may be surprised that a woman as lacking in self-control, as enthusiastic, and needy as St. Teresa is one of the women Doctors of the Church, as well as the recipient of some of the most exquisite graces.

This knowledge helps me to have hope that even I can be not only saved but also sanctified. How? Simply by openness to contemplative prayer. That prayer need not be performed in some perfect style but simply practiced in the natural way I would talk to any beloved person.

BEWAILING HER STATE OF IMPERFECTION

All mystics suffer greatly from what they regard as the mediocre state of their own souls. Teresa is particularly engaging in her sense of sin because she is so good at pinpointing the exact nature of her difficulties.

O life, life, where canst thou find thy sustenance when thou art absent from thy Life? In such great loneliness, how dost thou occupy thyself? What dost thou do, since all thy actions are faulty and imperfect?... I fear to live without serving Thee, yet when I set out to serve Thee I find no way of doing so that satisfies me or can pay any part of what I owe. I feel that I would gladly spend myself wholly in Thy service, and yet, when I consider my wretchedness, I realize that I can do nothing good unless Thou give it me....

What shall I do, so as not to destroy the effect of the wonders which Thou workest in me? Thy works are holy, just of inestimable worth and of great wisdom... but if my mind busies itself with this, my will complains, for it would have nothing hinder it from loving Thee.... The mind... desires to enjoy Him, yet knows not how, while confined within this grievous prison of mortality. Everything impedes it, though at first it was aided by meditation on Thy wonders, wherein it can the better see the baseness of numberless deeds of its own.

Why have I said this, my God? To whom can I complain?... My God, how shall I be sure that I am not separated from Thee? O my life, that must be lived in such uncertainty about a matter of such importance![5]

When I meditate, my God, upon the glory which Thou hast prepared for those who persevere in doing Thy will, and think how many trials and pains it cost Thy Son to gain it for us, and how little we had deserved it, and how bound we are not to be ungrateful for this wondrous love which has taught us love at such a cost to itself, my soul becomes greatly afflicted. How is it possible, Lord, that all this should be forgotten, and that, when they offend Thee, mortal men should be so forgetful of Thee? O my Redeemer, how forgetful are men! They are forgetful even of themselves.[6]

O my God and my Mercy! Now wilt Thou be able to show Thy mercies in Thy handmaiden! Powerful art Thou, great God. Now will it become clear, Lord, if my soul, looking upon the time it has lost, is right in its belief that Thou, in a moment, canst turn its loss to gain. I seem to be talking foolishly, for it is usual to say that time lost can never be recovered. Blessed be my God.[7]

What more do we want, Lord? What do we ask for? What do we seek? Why are worldly people lost if not because they are seeking repose? O God! O God! What is this, Lord? How sad a pity! How blind of us to seek repose where it cannot possibly be found! Have mercy, Creator, on these Thy creatures. Reflect that we do not understand ourselves, or know what we desire, nor are we able to ask as we should. Give us light, Lord. Behold, we need it more than the man who was blind from his birth, for he wished to see the light and could not, whereas nowadays, Lord, no one wishes to see it. Oh, what a hopeless ill is this! Here, my God, must be manifested Thy Power and Thy mercy.

Ah, how hard a thing am I asking of Thee, my true God! I ask Thee to love one who loves Thee not, to open to one who has not called upon Thee, to give health to one who prefers to be sick and who even goes about in search of sickness. Thou says, my Lord, that Thou comest to seek sinners; these, Lord, are the true sinners. Look not upon our blindness, my God, but upon all the blood that was shed for us by Thy Son. Let Thy mercy shine out amid such tremendous wickedness. Behold, Lord we are the works of Thy hands. Help us by Thy goodness and mercy.[8]

LOVE OF NEIGHBOR

We tend to think of love of neighbor as helping with physical needs. For this mystical soul, love often expresses itself more as friendship or prayer.

Often, my Lord, do I think that if life lived apart from Thee can find sustenance it will be in solitude, for there the soul rests with Him Who is its Rest indeed.... But how is it, my God, that rest itself is wearisome to the soul which strives after nothing but pleasing Thee?... Love of the world desires no companions, thinking that they may take from it what it possesses. But love for my God increases more and more as it learns that more and more souls love Him, just as its joys are dampened when it sees that all are not enjoying that same blessing. O my Good! Even during the greatest joys and delights which I experience in Thy company, I suffer at the thought of the many who do not desire these joys, and of those who will lose them for ever. And thus the soul seeks means of finding companionship and is glad to abandon its own enjoyment, thinking that this may help others in some degree to strive to attain it.[9]

O compassionate and loving Lord of my soul! Thou also sayest: "Come unto Me, all ye that thirst and I will give you to drink." How can anyone fail to have a great thirst who is consumed by living flames of covetousness for these miserable earthly things?... But if they have grown accustomed to living amid these flames, and are so inured to them that they cannot feel them, or ever realize the greatness of their need, what remedy is there for them, my God? ... See, my God, how much Thine enemies are gaining. Have compassion upon those who have none upon themselves; since their unhappy state prevents them from desiring to come to Thee, do Thou come to them, my God. I ask this of Thee in their name, and I know that when once again they return to their senses and realize their errors and begin to taste of Thee, they will rise again from the dead.[10]

Miserable creature though I am, I pray to Thee on behalf of those who will not pray to Thee themselves. Well knowest Thou, my King, how tormented I am to see them so forgetful of the great and endless torments which they will have to suffer if they turn not to Thee. Oh, you who are accustomed to delights and pleasures and comforts and to following your own will, take pity upon yourselves!... Not for a single moment are you sure of life: why, then, have you no desire to live for ever? O hardness of human hearts! May Thy boundless compassion soften them, my God.[11]

LONGING FOR ETERNITY

During her youth Teresa was once deathly ill, evidently falling into a coma that was mistaken for death. Wax was placed to close her eyes, but just before being buried, she woke up. Many asked her what death was like. Teresa used to say: "death is ecstasy." It seems as if this experience increased the longing shared by all mystics for an end to this earthly life so full of trials.

O my Joy, Lord of all things created and my God! How long must I wait before I shall see Thy Presence? What help canst Thou give to one who has so little on earth wherein she can find repose apart from Thee? O long life! O grievous life! O life which is no life at all! Oh, what utter, what helpless loneliness! When shall it end, then, Lord, when shall it end? How long shall it endure? What shall I do, my Good, what shall I do? Shall I perchance desire not to desire Thee? O my God and my Creator, Who doest wound and apply no remedy, dost strike so that no wound is seen, dost slay yet leave the slain with more life than before—Who, in short, my Lord, doest what Thou wilt as befits One full of power! Is it Thy will, then, my God, that so despicable a worm should suffer these conflicting distresses? Let it be so, my God, since Thou willest it so, for my only will is to love Thee.[12]

To those already saved in eternity: O souls that now rejoice without fear of losing your joy and are for ever absorbed in the praises of my God! Happy has been your lot! How right is it that you should employ yourselves ceaselessly in these praises and how my soul envies you, free as you now are from the affliction caused by the grievous offences which in these unhappy times are committed against my God!... O blessed, celestial souls! Help us in our misery and intercede for us with the Divine Mercy, so that we may be granted some part of your joy and that you may share with us some of that clear knowledge which is now yours.

Grant us, my God, to understand what it is that Thou givest to those who fight manfully through the dream of this miserable life. Help us, oh lover-souls, to understand what joy it gives you to behold the eternity of your bliss and what delight to possess with certain knowledge that it will never end. Oh, un-happy are we, my Lord, for well do we know and believe these truths; yet our inveterate habit of not reflecting upon them makes them so strange to our souls that they neither know them nor seek to know them![13]

Alas, alas, Lord! How long is this exile, and how, as I endure it, do I suffer, out of desire for my God! What can a soul do, Lord, when it is cast into this prison? O Jesus, how long man's life is, though we speak of it as short! Short it is, my God, for gaining life that cannot end, but very long for the soul that desires to see itself in the presence of its God. What cure canst Thou provide for this suffering? There is none, save to suffer for Thee.[14]

O life, that art the enemy of my welfare, would that one were permitted to end thee! I endure thee because God endures thee; I sustain thee because thou art His. Betray me not, be not ungrateful to me! And yet, Lord, alas, my exile is long; and time itself is short in exchange for Thine eternity; a sin-gle day, even an hour, is very long for one who knows not if he is offending Thee and fears lest he may do so. O free-will, thou art the slave of thine own freedom, unless thou be pierced through with fear and love for Him Who created thee! Oh, when will come that happy day in which thou shalt find thyself engulfed in that infinite ocean of supreme truth, wherein thou shalt not be free to sin, nor wish to be so, since thou shalt be secure from all misery, and made of one nature with the life of thy God!...

Blessed are those whose names are written in the book of that life. But if thou art among them, my soul, why art thou sad and why dost thou trouble me? Hope in God, for even now I will confess to Him my sins and His mercies and of them all I will make a song of praise and will breathe perpetual sighs to my Saviour and my God.... Rather would I live and die in the expectation and hope of eternal life than possess all created things and all the blessings which belong to them, since these must pass away.... Lord... do with me what Thou wilt.[15]

TRUST IN PROVIDENCE

In the midst of the weariness and miseries of this life, we must trust in God's providence, not only about exterior possessions but also about interior states of being that seem to contradict our glorious destiny.

But alas, alas, my Creator, great anguish makes me utter complaints and speak of that for which there is no remedy until Thou be pleased to send one. My imprisoned soul desires its freedom yet desires also not to swerve in the smallest degree from Thy will. Be pleased, my Glory, either to increase its affliction or to heal it altogether.... O my soul, let the will of thy God be done. It is well for thee that this should be so; serve Him and hope in His mercy, which will relieve thy affliction, when penitence for thy faults has won thee forgiveness for them: seek not fruition without having first suffered. O my true Lord and King, I am not fit even for this if I am not aided by Thy sovereign guidance and greatness, but with these I can do all things.[16]

Oh, oh, oh! How little do we trust Thee, Lord! How much greater were the riches and the treasures that Thou didst entrust to us! For our sakes—and all those years before we were born—Thou didst give Thy Son three and thirty years of grievous trials, followed by so unbearable and shameful a death. And, though knowing that we could not repay Thee, Thou didst not scruple to trust us with the inestimable treasure, in order on Thy side, merciful Father, to do everything to enable us to obtain from Thee what we win through Him.[17]

O true Lover! How pitifully, how gently, with what joy, with what comfort and with what exceeding great signs of love dost Thou heal these wounds that Thou hast inflicted with the arrows of love itself! O my God, and my Rest for all distress, how foolish I am! How could there be any human means of curing those stricken by the Divine fire?[18]

O my God and my infinite Wisdom, without measure and without bounds, high above the understanding both of angels and of men! O Love, Who lovest me more than I can love myself or conceive of love! Why, Lord, have I the will to desire more than it is Thy will to give me? Why do I wish to weary myself by begging Thee for things fashioned by my desire, since Thou already knowest what are the ends of all that my understanding can conceive and my will desire, while I myself know not what is best for me? The very thing in which my soul thinks to find profit will perchance bring about my ruin. For, if I beg Thee to deliver me from a trial, the object of which is my mortification, what is it that I am begging of Thee, my God? If I beseech Thee to give it to me, perchance it may not be proportionate to my patience, which is still weak and cannot bear so great a blow; and if I suffer it with patience and am not strong in humility, I may think that I have achieved something, whereas it is Thou that art achieving it all, my God.... No more trust in anything which I can desire for myself: do Thou desire for me that which Thou art pleased to desire; for that is my desire, since all my good consists in pleasing Thee.... Punish me not by giving me what I wish or desire, if Thy love desire not this.[19]

11

Saint Rosa of Lima
(1586–1617)

Ay Jesus de mi alma
Que bien pareces
Entre Flores y Rosas
Y Olivas Verdes

O Jesus my Savior
How wondrous your mien
Midst flowers and roses
And Olive trees green.[1]

✠ ✠ ✠

R OSA OF LIMA was the first canonized saint of the
Americas and was made patroness of all the
Americas, Philippine Islands, and India![2] Beautiful,
poetic, penitential in colorful rather than horrifying
ways, this charming woman was a mystic within the
familial setting. In the prayer-poem above, one finds
in the Spanish a play on her family names of Flores
and Oliva. Rosa was a nickname given the girl called

Isabel by her Indian nurse, who thought the child was as delicate and flower-like as a rose.

To understand Rosa's story we need to know a little bit about the period in which she lived. The city of Lima was founded in 1535 by Francisco Pizarro, a Spanish explorer seeking gold. In his greed, Pizarro ruthlessly destroyed defenseless and trusting Incas. The Spanish governors lived like European kings on the gold that was being mined. At the same time, many churches where built by pious Spaniards.

Rosa's father, Gaspar Flores, was a Puerto Rican soldier who came to Peru in 1548. Spain had by then reassumed authority over the country after the illegal reign of Gonzalo Pizarro. During this period of peace, when being a soldier was more of an honor than a dangerous charge, Gaspar Flores fell in love with Maria de Oliva, who was probably of mixed parentage—mostly Spanish and part Incan.

As a child, Rosa taught herself to read. Devout even as a little girl, she built herself a hermitage of leaves where she could find seclusion and pray earnestly from her heart. Early on the young saint embarked on a regimen of fasting and penance. From the standpoint of the family, Rosa's worst deed was to cut off her beautiful hair to avoid future suitors and pursue her vow of chastity.

In the manner of St. Francis of Assisi, Rosa loved flowers and animals. She liked to talk to birds and even to insects. Once when she knew that a bird she loved would be caught and cooked, she held it close to her heart and cajoled, "Sing, little bird, sing, if you don't wish to die." The bird saved itself by bursting into song.[3]

Here is her famous "mosquito tale" dating from later on in her life when she had become famous for her holiness:

Once, in the summertime, [a nobleman of Lima] went into the garden at the house of Rosa's parents, to see Rosa in her cell. He sat by the door in the shade of young trees. He and Rosa talked.... There were many mosquitoes bothering and biting him, but not one touched Rosa. Her face and hands were free of welts, too. He inquired, "My Mother, how is it that these mosquitoes bite guests and not my Mother?" Rosa replied,... "My Father, I have made friends with the mosquitoes ever since I've been coming to this cell; so, not only do they not bite me, but they are besides, for me, a great motive for praise of God. For by night, they gather here inside, and great swarms cling to the walls and when, by morning, I come and open the door, they rise, and I tell them we must praise the Lord. And really, my Father,... it seems the mosquitoes do just that, in concert of their humming."[4]

To return to Rosa's youthful days, the family was to experience quite a change of life style when her already elderly father was assigned to superintend the silver mines in Quives in the Andes. By then there were seven children. This move was quite a cross for Rosa's mother, who loved the luxurious life of Lima with its festivals and bullfights and religious processions.

In Quives, the young sensitive girl became personally acquainted with the resentment the subjugated Indian people felt toward the Spanish. After the family returned to Lima three years later, Rosa spent many years praying for these Indians and doing penance for their conversion. By the end of her life, many Indians of Lima came to visit her and receive her kindnesses.

By fourteen, we find Rosa refusing suitors attracted to her beauty and her sweet personality. Some of these became disciples when they realized that there was no turning her heart away from her interior bridegroom and toward themselves. The young woman was busy helping with the children and doing fine needlework to earn money for her family. Music and poetry were also natural expressions of her ethereal spirit.

Naturally, Rosa yearned to enter a convent where she could spend all day expressing her love for Jesus. But her mother was vexed by her daughter's religious ways. She loved Rosa passionately and could not bear to lose her to the Poor Clare convent. Claiming to need the money that she could earn from needlework, the mother dragged her away from the convent. She did promise that once home again, Rosa would be free to live in her hermitage, leaving this refuge only to sell flowers and go to Mass—where her daughter often remained in rapture for hours.

The decision to forego the life of a nun in favor of continuing at home was ratified by signs from the Virgin Mary. At twenty, Rosa became a Third Order Dominican, like so many other saints who were not allowed to become consecrated religious.

As a young girl Rosa had experienced great joy in her prayer, especially in her dialogues with her guardian angel whom she saw by her side constantly. However, once she had received the longed-for permission to retire to her cell in the garden for good, Rosa spent several years enduring the dark night of the soul. The saint slept less and less and ate hardly anything. For penance she scourged herself with a chain and wore an iron belt, the key to which she threw away in the well. A covering of roses surrounded her head, underneath which was a crown of thorns.

Many of Rosa's sufferings were offered for the souls in purgatory and the Indians. All this did not impede her from continuing her sewing, gardening, and tending poor children and sick elderly in an infirmary she set up within the large family house.

All these practices could not go unnoticed in a town as Catholic as Lima. In a time when false spiritualities were rampant, theologians were soon coming to question her. Rosa informed the professors that after her time of desolation was over, God entered her soul with a brilliant light, inflaming her with love and uniting her to Christ, and that she was always in his presence.

The investigators were very surprised that Rosa

had read nothing about mystical graces. Everything she knew about dogma had been taught her by God. They were even more astonished and awed when Rosa told them that she had never had to struggle with sin, since she always resisted the first movements of evil when they came into her thoughts. Christ often appeared to her in the form of a child, and Mary and her guardian angel were frequent companions. Rosa liked to say that God was "like ocean infinite or like infinite clouds."[5]

Her fame increased along with the gratitude of all those poor helped by her service. In a way Rosa initiated what would now be called social work. Because of these works of charity, this saint is hailed as the patroness of social workers in Peru. Rosa also became more well known to all the citizens of Lima when the city was besieged by pirates. Many fled in terror to the churches. Rosa left her home, not to hide, but to die in the sanctuary guarding the Blessed Sacrament. In a description based on contemporary accounts, Frances Parkinson Keyes paints the dramatic picture for us:

> Rosa mounted the altar steps and stood facing the door, which the pirates could be expected, at any moment, to force. She was enraptured with ecstasy [at the thought of being] her Saviour's crusader. And her guardian angel was at her side. The marauding band burst into the church and came charging up the aisle. Then, as suddenly as it had entered and advanced, it halted. The pirates did not even hear the crying children or see

the cowering women on either side of them. They saw only the figure of a slender girl, clad in black and white [the Third Order Dominican habit], her arms outstretched to shield the tabernacle, her face defiant, exalted and radiant.... There was a quality in it which was, at first, arresting, then blinding, then frightening. The pirates, despite their lust for loot and carnage, quailed before it. They would have said, indeed often had said, that they feared neither God nor man. But now they were afraid. They left the church as hastily as they had entered it. The next day their dark sails had disappeared beyond the horizon.[6]

St. Rosa of Lima died at the age of thirty-one after a sudden illness. She had predicted the time of her death as she told her family, "I am invited to a very great banquet tonight and surely I must go with great gladness." Hordes of people rich and poor honored her body as it was laid out for the funeral. Numerous miracles of healing took place. Rosa was beatified a mere fifty years after her death.

We do not have many prayers of St. Rosa, but we do have accounts of her infused graces and also some of her charming poetry. Why not ask the Holy Spirit to give you a lyrical spirit and write down the images that come to you, weaving together the fascination of nature with the deep feelings of your heart? If you let this happen, I believe you will find that both poetry and mysticism come forth from the same mansion of the soul, the one opening up the door to the other.

VISIONS AND PRAYERS OF ST. ROSA OF LIMA

I saw a great light which seemed a thing infinite and, in the midst of it, a rainbow, very beautiful and large, of many and varied tones, and above which there was another, equally beautiful, and above the second rainbow, I saw a cross whereon Jesus Christ had been crucified, and, under the first rainbow, I saw Our Lord Jesus Christ with such grandeur and majesty and beauty that I cannot, nor know how to explain.

And I saw Him face to face a very long while... face to face, all entire, from feet to head. And from His face and body, there came to my spirit and my body rays and tongues of glory so that I thought myself ended with this world and in glory itself.

A great number of angels came, very beautiful. They knelt to Him and did Him reverence. Afterwards, there came a great number of spirits.... I saw that Jesus Christ... distributed works and more works to the spirits. And I saw also that He imparted unto me a very great work.... [And then] he distributed to the spirits graces and more graces. And I saw that He imparted unto me more and more graces....

And Jesus Christ declared to me and said unto me, "May all know that, after works, comes grace, and that, without works, there is no grace; many works are necessary to augment it...."[7]

It seemed to her that the Divine Child, from the arms of His Mother, looked toward her with such infinite tenderness that Rosa was bathed in rapture.

"Rose of My Heart, be My spouse," she thought she heard Him say…. "Señor, I am only Your slave, ready to obey Your every command," she murmured. But Mary was confirming the words of the Saviour: "Rose, behold! My Son is showing you infinite mercy."[8]

Little singing nightingale, let us praise the Lord. Praise Thou thy creator, while I praise my redeemer.[9]

Prayer to St. Dominic, when Rosa was told in prayer of her approaching death:
Padre, my mother
Will be alone
Please be her comforter
When I am gone.[10]

Prayer to her guardian angel:
Fly, O swift messenger,
Fly to Our Lord!
Oh, haste to our dear Master adored!
Ask why He delays, and remains
Far from our side.

Tell Him I cannot live
Parted from Him:
My life then no happiness knows:
in Him only my heart can repose,
Or pleasure can find.

Fly noble messenger, fly!
Tell Him when he is not here
I languish alone.
Tell Him His Rose must her sorrow bemoan
Till the moment when he shall return.[11]

12

Blessed Marie of the Incarnation
(1599–1672)

I dreamed of a very beautiful place. Here there was a man garbed in white, in clothes resembling those in which the Apostles are depicted... indicating with a gesture that we must go the way he pointed.... We reached our destination, and I entered with a companion. It was a beautiful place with no covering but the sky.... It was very silent there and that was part of its beauty.... On my right, was a little church of white marble, constructed in a pretty, ancient style. On top of the pinnacle was a chair in which the Blessed Virgin was seated, holding her little Jesus in her lap with her arms around him. The place was very elevated and beneath it lay a great, vast country, full of mountains and valleys and thick fog.... The Blessed Virgin, Mother of God, gazed at this country which aroused as much compassion as fear.... I ran toward the Divine Mother, holding out my arms, so that they could touch both sides of this little church on which she was seated.... I felt that she spoke to him of this country and of me and that she had some plan for me.... With endearing grace she turned toward

me, and with a smile full of love kissed me without say-
ing a word.[1]

❈ ❈ ❈

I N THIS MANNER DID GOD intimate to one of his chosen mystical women the apostolic journey from
France to Canada which was to crown her many fascinating adventures in grace.

Blessed Marie of the Incarnation is an important
witness in the history of contemplative prayer for
many reasons. First of all, she was a wife, mother, and
business woman—ways of life that some imagine
incompatible with the mystical path. What is more,
Marie's special graces of prayer came after she was
widowed. They were not designed to lead her into
the cloister but instead into the dangerous life of a
missionary.

However, the scenes of Marie's life that most delight me do not involve her heroic vocation as an
evangelist to Canadian Indians threatened by war-
ring tribes. Rather I am struck by the time when she
was helping her relatives run their carting business
and somehow managing to enjoy mystical visions
while watering down the horses!

But let's go back to the beginning. Marie of the
Incarnation was born as Marie Guyart, the daughter
of a middle-class family of bakers in the French city
of Tours. (She is not to be confused with the other
famous French Marie of the Incarnation, Madame
Acarie.) At the age of seven, our little Marie was ush-
ered into union with Christ by a vivid dream:

I saw Our Lord Jesus Christ in human form emerge and come toward me... the most beautiful of all the children of men, took me in his arms and with a look full of indescribable sweetness and charm, kissed me with great love and asked me, "Will you be mine?" I answered, "Yes."[2]

Although somewhat drawn to the life of a nun, Marie assented to her parents' judgment that she was made for a practical life in the world as the wife of Claude Martin, a merchant of the city. At eighteen she became the mother of a son; less than a year afterwards her husband died. Having a very practical side to her character, Marie did not let her husband's business sink into bankruptcy. She decided to rescue it. It was then that she experienced what some would call her adult conversion:

[One] morning on my way to work I was earnestly commending my business affairs to God with my usual prayer: "In Thee, O Lord, I have put my trust; let me never be disappointed."... Then, in an instant, my inner eyes were opened and all the faults, sins, and imperfections that I had committed since my birth were shown to me in the most vivid detail.... At the same moment I saw myself immersed in the blood of the Son of God, shed because of the sins which had been shown to me. ... I think I would have died of terror had God's goodness not sustained me, so frightful and shocking is the sight of sin, no matter how slight.[3]

Marie experienced for a time a profusion of illuminative graces, pouring into her soul not only when she was alone but also right in the middle of directing the stevedores in unloading the ships at the docks. When they discovered her natural gifts for supervisory work, her sister and brother-in-law soon cajoled her into taking over the business for them.

During the time before Marie withdrew from the world to become an Ursuline nun, she was given the mystical insights into the meaning of redemption, the Sacred Heart, the Eucharist, and the Holy Trinity —truths that were to be the framework for her later missionary labors. All of this interior wealth culminated in the mystical marriage:

> ... the Sacred Person of the Divine Word revealed to me that he was in truth the spouse of the faithful soul.... At that moment, this adorable Person seized my soul and embracing it with indescribable love, united it to himself, taking it as his spouse.[4]

The closer her union with God, the more Marie longed for a consecrated life, far from the trivia of daily business. On the other hand she did not know how to resolve the question of her greatly loved son, not yet a teenager and extremely attached to his mother. At the age of thirty-one, she received continual leadings in prayer that God wanted her in the religious life. In those days of extended family life, her director gave Marie permission to entrust her son to her relatives and become an Ursuline teaching sister. This vocation attracted her because of her concern for the salvation of souls.

When the time came to enter the convent, the emotional wrenching was almost unbearable on both sides. Marie's son—who was later to become a holy priest totally reconciled to the wisdom of his mother's dedication and continually united with her in mystical prayer—found the break devastating. He tore his mother's heart to pieces by screaming outside the convent walls that he wanted his mother back. Marie's biographer, Irene Mahoney, is convinced that the severe depression Marie experienced after her original ecstasy wore off was caused by the painful separation from her son.[5]

Marie was finally liberated from depression by the French mission venture to Canada, prefigured in the mystical dream described in the opening of this chapter. She was chosen by the Jesuit missionaries as the ideal sister to minister to the Indians of the Quebec region, who needed not only priests but also the motherly care of Catholic sisters. After three months of misery on the ocean voyage, Marie found herself in the land of forests and mountains pictured in her dream.

Once settled in, she had to face conditions of drastic poverty, freezing cold, wars where violent tribes killed the Indians converted by the Jesuits, and fires that destroyed the houses they would build. Only her tremendous love for Christ and her maternal love for the children made such a life bearable. Her daily routine would include washing the chil-

dren and combing their hair, teaching, learning
Indian languages, and administering to her small
band of sisters.

Worst of all, the sisters were faced with trying to
overcome the sins of the French soldiers who undid
their work with the sale of alcohol. Ultimately the
sisters would become more involved in the formation of the French girls of colonial families through
the establishment of schools than in their original
work with the Indians. Here is the description Marie
gives of her life at the mission:

> People who came to visit us could not understand
> how we could embrace these little orphans, hold-
> ing them in our laps, when their bodies were
> heavily smeared with grease [to protect against
> the cold] and covered only by a small greasy rag.
> For us all this was an unimaginable happiness....
> I carry them all in my heart and try very gently
> through my prayers to win them for heaven.[6]

Three features especially characterize the spirituality of Marie of the Incarnation. First, she demon-
strated a clear theological framework with special
emphasis on God's glory in the Holy Trinity. Second,
Marie's interior graces overflowed in her active missionary work. Third, she thirsted for purification
through suffering as the only authentic path to
supernatural joy. The following quotations reflect
these aspects of Marie's spiritual way:

> I saw everything beneath God as narrow and lim-
> ited. Blinded by the sight of this infinite being, I

was happy and took pleasure in the fact that nothing can penetrate the depths of this abyss of majesty... and I said over and over: Lord who is like to you?[7]

... During this union I experienced a strong desire that the many souls who do not belong to the Church, and so many others who do belong but who are not in the state of grace would be sincerely converted.[8]

After the terrible suffering of the first three years [of life in Canada] I continued to suffer for another four from a bitterness aimed at some good and holy people... whenever anything arises capable of stirring antipathy or aversion. I shall never grow weary of repeating that this is the most painful thing in the world for a soul who fears God and sin and who loves purity of heart.... The soul is desperately afraid of being deluded. [Since it appears to have so little love of neighbor] it believes it has never had any solid virtue. Whatever it thought to have received interiorly it now feels has not come from God.[9]

Yet in her last letter to a Jesuit priest in 1670 she could write the following:

Yet God makes all this [all her faults] compatible with a state of union which has kept me bound to his Divine Majesty for several years without deviating from it a single moment.... During this period God shines at the depth of the soul, which is, as it were, in waiting, like a person whom one interrupts while he is speaking to another and who, nevertheless, still maintains the sight of the person to whom he is talking. The soul, as it were, waits in silence before returning to its intimate union.... The effects of this state are peace of heart in temporal events and the desire to want only what God wants in all the effects of his divine providence as they occur from moment to moment.[10]

The prayers I have excerpted from the writings of Blessed Marie of the Incarnation are from *Notes from a Ten-Day Retreat*.[11] Each prayer arises from meditation on the particular passage from Scripture cited beforehand. As you read the prayers, you might ask God to expand your own heart beyond the confines of daily troubles. Ask him to give you a heart which aches for the salvation of souls, especially those of your loved ones and friends.

GOD'S GRANDEUR AND MAJESTY

Many a spiritual director tries to convince his or her advisees that it is better to avoid concentration on the state of one's own soul in favor of the balm of wonder, awe, and adoration of God. Such prayer of praise does not consist in many words but in simple and elevating aspirations.

His majestic glory their eyes behold; his glorious voice their ears heard. (Sirach 17:7, 11)

O great abyss, how captivating are your charms!

May you be blessed, O my great abyss, O abyss of goodness.[12]

How deep are the riches and the wisdom and the knowledge of God! How inscrutable his judgments, how unsearchable his ways. (Romans 11:33)

At that very moment when I recalled the divine perfections, I found myself in a state of infinity where there were neither boundaries nor limits, and inwardly I cried in admiration: O Height! O Depths! O Greatness.[13]

Let not the wise man glory in his wisdom, nor the strong man glory in his strength, nor the rich man in his riches but let him glory in knowing me. (Jeremiah 9:23)

I was caught up in a great joy and an unparalleled happiness in having within me the source of my glory and in seeing that the true cause of my glory is to know God and to recognize him by faith.... This deep-seated joy was followed by a completely new kind of love, resulting from the details of this heavenly knowledge of which the divine goodness has given me so wonderful a share.... Glorying in knowing him, I said: Let the wise not glory in their wisdom, for the demons are wiser than they; let the strong not glory in their strength, animals are stronger than men; let not the rich glory in their riches, for sinners are generally richer than good people; but those who wish to glory, let them glory in the knowledge and recognition of God. There will be found my glory and my honor.[14]

His servants shall no longer need the light of lamp or sun, for the Lord God will give them light and they shall reign forever. (Revelation 22:5)

My soul was united to this incomprehensible light which, nevertheless, seemed to me like darkness although I saw quite clearly that it was indeed light and a light at once incomprehensible, immense, and infinite. Then I said, "O my great God, thus it will be that I will see you eternally in the splendors of your majesty, that I shall be lost forever in the abyss of your lights; thus forever will I find you in yourself to enjoy the grandeurs of your glory and to reign with your servants forever and ever."[15]

RELYING ON GOD ALONE

Some Christians try to substitute all sorts of techniques for true, humble prayer. In the end, we have only hope in God to sustain us, so let us always turn to him first.

Live on in me, as I do in you. No more than a branch can bear fruit of itself apart from the vine, can you bear fruit apart from me. (John 15:4)

At my first glance at this passage my will was drawn to God by a yearning of love, saying to him: "It is true, my Beloved, it is true. May I remain in you and you in me." In the union which I experienced with the divine majesty, there was a light which let me see what it is to be grafted into God through Jesus Christ and also what it is to be separated from him.... These lights moved my will to plunge deeper and deeper into its divine object, asking that these words become effective: "Remain in me and I in you." I begged that they would have the same effect in my soul as they had had in the Apostles, who would have been able to do nothing without his spirit and the strengthening power of his love. I said to the Eternal Father: "O divine Father, please give me this faith which will unite me to your Son and make me one body with him;... Please give me those daily graces necessary to be fruitful in virtue and good works."[16]

All that is mine is thine and what is thine is mine and I will be glorified in them. (John 17:10)

Glorify yourself in me and triumph over her who belongs to you because my glory consists in belonging to you and you to me. Everything you have is mine. You have given me a part of it and have led me to hope for the rest. And all that I have is yours, for I have nothing I have not received from you and I wish for nothing except for you.... How could all that I have not be yours since I am yours, given to you as an irrevocable and perpetual holocaust?[17]

I remember God and the joys I have had. I meditate and my spirit faints. (Psalm 72:4)

My spirit no sooner glanced at this subject than my soul was caught up in an extraordinary joy at the thought that God is the inexhaustible source of the pleasures of our eternal happiness and that nothing beneath him can ever satisfy it.... In the ardor of its longing, my will said with the prophet: "My soul is thirsting for the living God; when shall I go and appear before the face of the Lord?"... "When shall

I drink of the river which gladdens your holy city? Of the torrent of delight that you give to your blessed?" In the sight of these eternal joys both my understanding and my will slipped into a trance, powerless either to act or to desire: the first having reached the perfection of its knowledge; and the latter the goal of its desires.

Nevertheless, during this period of passivity I longed to speak and I managed to do so—but only half-words uttered in a broken voice. What I wanted to show Our Lord was that I wanted neither joy nor consolation nor happiness except in him, as he is in himself and in his glory. Thus I said to him: "You understand, O Love, you understand." Then words failed me completely and I remained in this silence.[18]

13

Blessed Mary of Agreda
(1602–1665)

I again remind those who shall read this history not to be astonished at the hidden (matters) recorded of the most blessed Mary therein, nor to hold them unworthy of belief, because they have not been until now revealed to the world.... They are all worthy and befitting this great Queen.[1]

✠ ✠ ✠

B LESSED MARY OF AGREDA was born in Spain in 1602, one of the most well-read and beloved mystics of church history.[2] At fifteen Mary entered a convent of cloistered discalced Franciscan nuns in Agreda of the province of Burgos. She was given the name Sister Mary of Jesus.

Against all her humble protestations, Sister Mary was very early chosen as abbess and re-elected over and over again during her long life. So famous did she become for her visions that King Philip IV used to consult her about political affairs. The father and mother of Blessed Mary entered religious life around the year 1617 as well as two brothers and a sister.

Blessed Mary of Agreda is still so well-known for two main reasons. The first concerns one of the most miraculous events in the history of evangelism. Many years before the arrival of missionaries to the areas now known as Arizona and New Mexico, the Indians were evangelized and catechized by a Franciscan nun. From the drawings made of this nun, later missionaries could easily identify her as none other than Blessed Mary of Agreda—who had never left Spain! The miracle was inferred to have taken place through bilocation![3]

The other reason for the renown of Mary of Agreda is her prodigious work entitled the *Mystical City of God*, a four-volume compendium of visions and locutions received by the Franciscan nun from the Virgin Mary, Jesus, and other supernatural agencies. She describes the origin of these books in this way:

Ever since I have had the use of reason, I was conscious of especially one blessing... a great and penetrating fear lest I should lose Him [God].... On account of this dread... I have in these latter times begun to send up earnest and heartfelt prayers and petitions to the Lord, asking also the intercession of the Queen and Virgin, that I may be guided and led along the secure paths hidden from the eyes of men.... And presently I felt a change within me and a highly spiritualized state of mind. To my understanding was given a new light, which illuminated it and infused into it a knowledge of all things in God.... It is a knowledge of light, holy, sweet, and pure, subtle, penetrating, sure and agile, causing love of good and hatred of evil. It is the breath of the power of God and an emanation of a most subtle light, which acts as a mirror for my understanding. Thus the higher faculties and the interior perception of my soul began to expand in their activity....[4]

The introduction of the *Mystical City of God* includes the many words Our Lady spoke to give Blessed Mary the courage to begin, continue, and rewrite this gigantic work of love. So afraid was she of the censure that might come if she were to be judged to be a presumptuous fraud, that she once burned up the entire manuscript.

Blessed Mary's introduction goes on to describe several levels of communication from supernatural sources. Her account shows that she herself recognized that on the lower levels of perception and writing she could very well have introduced into the text materials about which she is not absolutely sure of the source. Reading her sober analysis is a help to readers who might otherwise decide to abandon their meditative reading whenever they come upon some scientific explanation no longer considered valid in our times.

The introduction, written by the translator Fiscar Marison, contained a necessary caveat about private revelation. As you probably know already, no one is obliged by the authority of the church to believe any revelation made to anyone after the canon of the Scriptures was fixed. However, when not disapproved by appropriate hierarchy, such revelations may be used in meditation with great benefit.[5] In fact, after initial mockery, the *Mystical City of God* was given approval by many popes. Its fame and acclaim spread rapidly in many translations all over the world.

Even as far back as 1902, Fiscar Marison thought it important to add this note to his prefatory remarks:

> It does seem that He [God] prefers women for private revelation. He chose men to reveal the great public truths of the Bible and to attend to the public teaching, but to women in the new law He seems to have consigned the task of private revelations.... In fact, no special learning or great natural insight is required of a messenger; such qualities might tend to corrupt or narrow down the inspired message to mere human proportions.... Humility, great piety and love, deep faith are the requisites of God's special messengers. Women as a rule are more inclined to these virtues than men, and therefore are not so apt to trim the message of God down to their own natural powers of understanding.[6]

The four-volume work is divided into these titles comprising salvation history: The Conception, The Incarnation, the Transfixion, and the Coronation. Of great interest is the living narration of events and interior sentiments in the life of the Blessed Mother. The visions and locutions seem to be real rather than fanciful. They very dramatically help us to understand how Mary must have felt year by year as the astounding events in the life of her Son unfolded.

Blessed Mary Agreda's personal prayers are less significant in church history than her account of locutions and visions. I have therefore chosen to focus on her description of Mary's life and sufferings. No human person was closer to Jesus than his Mother. We need to come close to her as a model and intercessor so that the salvation won for us by the blood of the Savior may not be lost to us out of carelessness or despair.

Quite a number of accounts of the life of Jesus and Mary have been written by visionaries. Though some contemporary ones are easier to read, the four-volume *Mystical City of God* and its smaller condensation to one volume are surely among the most theologically sublime and make excellent spiritual reading.

MARY'S CONCEPTION AND YOUTH

Concerning the plan for Mary's conception: As the opportune and pre-ordained time had arrived, the three divine Persons conferred with each other saying: "Now is the time to begin the work of our pleasure and to call into existence that pure Creature and that soul, which is to find grace in our eyes above all the rest. Let Us furnish her with the richest gifts and let Us deposit in her the great treasures of our grace. Since all others, whom We called into existence, have turned out ungrateful and rebellious to our wishes, frustrating our intention and impeding by their own fault our purpose, namely, that they conserve themselves in the happy state of their first parents... let Us therefore create this being in entire sanctity and perfection, so that the disorder of the first sin shall have no part in Her. Let Us create a soul according to our pleasure, a fruit of our attributes, a marvel of our infinite power.... Let her be a most special image and likeness of our Divinity and let her be in our presence for all eternity the culmination of our good will and pleasure."[7]

Sister Mary asked the Virgin if she had to go through the same humiliating physical weaknesses of all other children: "My daughter, since thou art full of wonder, I will inform thee in all kindness. It is true that I was in possession of grace and the use of reason from the first instant of my conception.... I underwent the hardships of infancy as other children and I was reared and treated as others in the same condition. I felt hunger, thirst, sleepiness and other infirmities of the body, and as a daughter of Adam I was subject to these accidental necessities; for it was just that I should imitate my most holy Son, who subjected Himself to these hardships and defects.... I felt less the want of sleep on account of the opportunity which it furnished me for the presence and the heavenly conversation of the angels."[8]

Concerning the council of devils responding to their knowledge that Mary was the woman prophesied to defeat them: In his restless fury [the ancient serpent] called a conventicle of the infernal leaders in order to consult about the matter.... "The great triumph which we have until now obtained in the world by the possession of so many souls who are altogether subject to our wills, is, I am afraid and anxious, about to be undone and counteracted by a Woman.... Therefore we must be watchful and discard all carelessness.... I have not been able to discover in her the effects of the seeds of malice.... I have always seen her composed and most perfect, without being able to incline or induce her to fall into the slightest human imperfections, which are so natural in the other children.... I desire the destruction of this soul more than that of all the world...." But the divine power, which overshadowed her, hindered the assaults of Lucifer, so that he could not approach very closely to her.[9]

MARY'S PRAYER LIFE

Locution of the Virgin Mary: "My admonition to thee, whom in spite of thy weakness and poverty I have chosen with such generous kindness as my disciple and companion, is this: that thou strive with all thy powers to imitate me in an exercise in which I persevered during my whole life from the very first moment of my birth, omitting it on not a single day, however full of cares and labors it might have been. This exercise was the following: every day at beginning of dawn, I prostrated myself in the presence of the Most High and gave Him thanks and praise for his immutable Being, his infinite perfections, and for having created me out of nothing.... I raised up my spirit to place it into his hands, offering myself with profound humility and resignation to him and asking him to dispose of me according to his will during that day and during all the days of my life, and to teach me to fulfill whatever would be to his greater pleasure. This I repeated many times during the external works of the day, and in the internal ones I first consulted his majesty, asking his advice, permission and benediction for all my actions."[10]

Locution concerning God's direction of Mary's hopes: The Most High urged her with great benevolence, that from now on she would many times each day pray for the hastening of the Incarnation of the eternal Word and for the Redemption of all the human race, and that She should bewail the sins of men, which impede their salvation and restoration.[11]

Mary's prayer after the Ascension: "I desire, seek and solicit thy greater pleasure and satisfaction, thy greater glory and the exaltation of thy name in the holy Church.... I desire also that the Apostles commence even now to consecrate the body and the blood of thy and my Son, in order that by this new and admirable sacrifice they may give Thee praise and thanks for the blessing of the Redemption and all the favors Thou has through it conferred upon the world, and also that according to thy will the children of the Church may in it receive the nourishment of eternal life."[12]

After Pentecost: She did not rest or lose one moment or occasion of conferring some singular favor either upon the whole Church or some of its members. For she consumed herself either in praying and beseeching her divine Son... or in exhorting, instructing, counseling, and, as Treasurer and Dispenser of the divine favors, distributing graces in diverse manners among the children of the Gospel.... She saw and knew us all in the order and succession in which we were to be born in the Church; and she prayed and interceded for us no less than for those who lived in her times.... She exhorted and animated the Apostles and the ministers of the divine word, fixing their attention upon the prodigious manifestation of the divine power, by which her most holy Son began to plant the faith of his Church; the virtue which the Holy Ghost had communicated to them in order to make them fit ministers; the ever present assistance of the divine right hand.... She broke forth in canticles of praise and exultation.... She received all, listened to all, and endeared herself to them with words of light and life.[13]

MARY'S SUFFERINGS

Concerning Mary's fear that she had lost her Son during their trip to Jerusalem: Her anxiety of heart caused her to break out in tears and sighs of inmost grief....She persevered in her tears and groans without cessation or rest, without sleeping or eating anything for three whole days. Although the... angels accompanied her in corporeal forms and witnessed her affliction and sorrow, yet they gave her no clue to find her lost child.... For the loss of Jesus was greater to her than the loss of anything created, while her love and appreciation of Him exceeded all that can be conceived by any other creature.... Moreover, during these three days the Lord... suspended all the other consolations and blessings so constantly vouchsafed to her most holy soul.[14]

Mary's participation in the sufferings of Jesus in the agony of the garden: Mary left her retreat in order to meet him on the way. At this face to face meeting of the Prince of eternity and of the Queen, a sword of sorrow pierced the heart of Son and mother, inflicting a pang of grief beyond all human and angelic thought. The sorrowful mother threw herself at the feet of Jesus, adoring him as her true God and Redeemer. The Lord, looking upon her with a majesty divine and at the same time with the overflowing love of a son, spoke to her only these words: "My mother, I shall be with thee in tribulation; let us accomplish the will of the eternal Father and the salvation of men." The great Queen offered herself as a sacrifice with her whole heart and asked his blessing. Having received this she returned to her retirement, where, by a special favor of the Lord, she was enabled to see all that passed in connection with her divine Son.[15]

At the foot of the cross: When the mother perceived that now the mysteries of the Redemption were to be fulfilled and that the executioners were about to strip Jesus of his clothes for crucifixion, she turned in spirit to the eternal Father and prayed as follows: "... as man he was born of my womb and received from me this human nature, in which he now suffers. I have nursed and sustained him at my own breast; and as the best of sons that ever can be born of any creature, I love him with maternal love. As his mother I have a natural right in the Person of his most holy humanity.... This right of a mother then, I now yield to thee and once more place in thy hands thy and my Son as a sacrifice for the Redemption of man."[16]

14

Saint Margaret Mary Alacoque
(1647–1690)

My divine heart is so impassioned with love for men and for you in particular that, unable any longer to contain the flames of its burning charity, they must be spread abroad by you.[1]

✠ ✠ ✠

O F THE MANY SAINTS who promoted devotion to the Sacred Heart, the most well-known of the women is St. Margaret Mary Alacoque, a seventeenth-century Visitation Sister. Because of the sentimental tone of some devotional literature, I always thought that Margaret Mary was among the sweeter simpler saints—one whom I dearly love but / never quite identify with. What a surprise!

Her story starts conventionally enough, b ceeds along quite unexpected pathways. was born in 1647 in Burgundy, France, child in a family of seven children. She inative and merry girl, as well as very garet's mother was a dear womar capable. Everyone therefore thought it a very good idea when Margaret's godmother took the four-year-old to live with her in her large house because she was lonely and had plenty of servants.

This beautiful home included a chapel where the Blessed Sacrament was always reserved. Although generally a high-spirited child, one thing about little Margaret was very surprising to the servants. She loved to visit the chapel and kneel there for hours without moving! She was only eight years old when she felt led to repeat the vow over and over: "Oh my God, I dedicate to You my purity and I make to You a vow of perpetual chastity."[2]

When her godmother died, Margaret returned to her own house, but shortly afterwards, her father died. The family was left in poverty when they discovered that he had been extravagant in his expenditures. The children were sent off to religious schools and Margaret went to a convent school. The sisters soon noticed that this girl who was so rowdy at games loved to pray before the Blessed Sacrament. Often she would interrupt play to run to the chapel or to hide in some small corner.

This pleasant life underwent an abrupt change when Margaret came down with rheumatic fever, leaving her bedridden for four years. During this time she made a vow that if the Blessed Virgin cured her she would one day become one of her daughters. After this promise, Margaret was healed. It seemed to her that the Blessed Virgin taught her by day how to do God's will.

But then came fresh trials. Various relatives had taken over the Alacoque household to substitute for the deceased father and the weak-willed mother. They refused to let Margaret go to Mass during the week, assuming that such trips must be pretexts for meeting boyfriends.

To compensate, Margaret spent ten years hiding in the fields and gazing at the church where she knew her beloved Christ was to be found inside the tabernacle. This description seems particularly moving to me. Most of us do not act out our longing for the Eucharistic Christ in such a visible way, but which of us has not felt a similar nostalgia for God as the home of our hearts, so much better than our own.

When not in hiding, Margaret spent her time in the house nursing her sick mother. Happily, this rather introverted routine changed when her oldest brother came back home and took over the estate again. The reserved young woman suddenly blossomed and became popular with the young people of the village. She was charming and lively and would receive a good dowry when she would marry.

One day while praying her rosary, Margaret had a vision of Mary reproaching her for having forgotten her vow. In fact, she was torn between her love of pleasure and her love for God. This love drew her to prayer, though she had no idea how to develop this leaning into a deeper form of contemplation.

Meanwhile Margaret's widowed mother implored her to marry so that she, the mother, would have a place to settle down in peace with her favorite child.

So Margaret went to the usual dances for young people in order to please her. In the middle of such amusements, she would feel Jesus shooting arrows into her heart to draw her back into prayer.[3] By means of visions and locutions, Jesus would tell her that it was her vanity which had been part of his own pain at Calvary.

Touched to the core, Margaret would long for her true bridegroom, especially in the form of Holy Communion. After receiving the Lord, she would be in ecstasy without speaking and eating, seeking only solitude. Finally her family allowed her to become a nun. At twenty-two she entered the Visitation convent of Paray-le-Monial. "I felt like a slave freed from prison and chains to enter the house of her Beloved, to take possession of it, to rejoice, absolutely free, in His presence, His riches and His love."[4]

Once enclosed, Margaret devoted herself to prayer and penance. One day while praying in the chapel, Margaret Mary heard the Lord inviting her to take the place of St. John the Evangelist close to his Sacred Heart and to spread such devotion so that all Catholics would know of his great love for them.[5] This was at a time when many French people were caught up in Jansenism, a heresy which emphasized God's judgment to the neglect of his mercy. Many Catholics frequented Holy Communion but rarely. Some church historians regard devotion to the Sacred Heart as the remedy of the Holy Spirit for this spirit of Jansenism.[6]

For eighteen months, Margaret Mary continued to experience special revelations. When she described them to her superior, this nun thought that the experiences were not authentic. The sensitive Margaret Mary was devastated by this rejection. Soon many of her sisters were looking at her askance as the nun who was deluded. Then Margaret Mary became very ill. The superior thought that perhaps her harsh judgments had made the younger nun sick and vowed that if she recovered, she would take it as a sign that the visions were valid.

When Margaret Mary got better, the superior sent for some theological experts to investigate whether the mystical experiences were truly from God or not. These judges rejected her story. When the Jesuit priest who was finally to accept her accounts and help her propagate the devotion to the Sacred Heart arrived as a chaplain to the convent, the desperate sister shrank from contact and refused to open her heart.

Eventually, Blessed Claude de la Colombière, S.J., won her heart and was able to spread the devotion not only throughout France but also to England, and finally through writing to all the world. Since 1929, the feast of the Sacred Heart has been elevated to the highest rank, and many contemporary Catholics believe that the consecration of the family to the Sacred Heart has been the greatest cause of their perseverance.

The last words of St. Margaret Mary at her death-bed in 1690 were these: "I need nothing but God, and to lose myself in the heart of Jesus."[6] When we fall in love, we feel as if we have given the key to our heart to another. In exchange, we feel that person has given us a heart where we are free to roam about at will and be comforted by a warmth familiar but different, new, enlivening. So it is with our God of love. He wants us to feel utterly free to hide in his wounded heart. Let us not cling to some false stoic self-sufficiency, but come to him with the trust of St. Margaret Mary.

THE SACRED HEART

We all long for a perfectly reciprocated love. Are we afraid to ask Christ for the intimacy we seek?

He asked for my heart which I begged Him to take, as he did, and placed it in His adorable one, in which He showed it to me as a tiny speck consumed in this burning furnace. Then, taking it out as a burning flame shaped like a heart He replaced it from the place from which He had taken it.[7]

Behold this Heart which has so loved men, has spared nothing, even to suffering and death, to show them its love and instead of gratitude I receive for the most part nothing but ingratitude, irreverence and sacrilege, the coldness and contempt which they show to me in this sacrament of love.[8]

SUFFERING

Closeness coming from continual dialogue with Christ makes it possible to see suffering in a different way.

About the time she was bedridden with terrible pain as a young girl for four years: Oh, my God, I did not think then what You have made me know and experience since, that Your Sacred Heart, having brought me to birth on Calvary with so much suffering, the life you have given could only sustain itself by the food of the Cross.[9]

My sovereign Master showed me that my soul was the blank canvas on which he wished to paint all the details of His life of suffering, entirely spent in love and poverty, solitude, silence and sacrifice till the end. That he would so stamp my soul after having cleansed from it all the stains still on it, as much with affection for earthly things as love of myself and creatures, toward which my self-satisfied nature tended. In that moment He deprived me of everything and, after emptying my heart and stripping my soul naked, he lit in it so burning a desire to love and suffer that it gave me no rest.[10]

SURRENDER

In response to the God who abandons himself to us and offers us his heart so vulnerably, we must abandon ourselves in utter trusting love.

May I no longer live save by Thee and for Thee. Be then my life, my love, my all.[11]

I offer, dedicate and consecrate wholly and inviolate to the Sacred Heart of adorable Jesus all the merit to be acquired or given during life and after death that the will of the Divine Heart dispose of them as He will.[12]

Blessed Mariam Baouardy
(1846–1878)

There was a large round flowerbed; this round area had several circumferences within it. The first was all planted with roses: the rose stands for charity and the thorn for vigilance. The second circuit was covered with vines, whose grapes represent love and their leaves gentleness. The third was planted with wheat, which signifies confidence and hope. The center was covered with violets which stand for true humility. And, in the middle, I set up a throne and had Jesus sit down. And, under His feet, a spring gushed forth which said: Everything passes, everything flows by like water. Beside the throne I planted pansies and some ivy. The ivy said: Constantly hold fast to Jesus. And the pansies told me: Think only of Jesus. Lord Jesus, plant all these virtues in the depths of my heart, and make them increase yourself by your power. [1]

❈ ❈ ❈

THE STORY OF Blessed Mariam, also called the Little Arab, is so extraordinary as to invite disbelief. As you read the narrative of her life, please be reassured that the writer of the standard biography in English insists on the veracity of all that is recorded. Ample documentation is given, including reference to the information compiled in the Vatican archives needed to postulate the cause of Mariam's beatification.[2]

Mariam Baouardy was born in Galilee in 1846 to a family of Lebanese origin from the Greek-Melkite Catholic Rite. Her birth was supernatural in its circumstances, for her parents had previously had twelve sons, all of whom died in infancy. After the death of the twelfth, her mother decided to make a pilgrimage on foot to Bethlehem to beg the Virgin Mary for a daughter. This daughter was Mariam. After Mariam's birth, they had a son, Paul, but both parents died soon after and Mariam was taken in by an uncle.

As a young girl Mariam was very dreamy and thoughtful, always looking for ways to be alone with God. She was not taught to read or write but only the duties of a future wife and mother. The family moved to Alexandria. When Mariam was thirteen, the Lord came to her in a vision and promised her that he would make it possible for her to be his bride instead of being given in marriage.

Not accepting this visitation as real, Mariam's relatives betrothed her and decked her out in wedding clothing for the marriage. To avoid this fate Mariam cut off her hair and refused to be wed. (Sometimes I think someone could start up a thriving wig shop making use of the hair of future women saints!)

The family was not pleased with Mariam's deci-

sion. They punished her by making her work as a
servant. Seeing how badly she was treated, a former
Moslem servant befriended the girl and brought her
to his house to serve under better conditions. His
real intention, however, was to convert Mariam to
Islam. When she refused he slashed her throat and
left her in an alley to die!

Mariam later told her mistress of novices that she
had died and been taken to heaven, but then instructed to return to earth. A mysterious woman
who Mariam was convinced was the Virgin Mary herself nursed the injured girl for a month and then
brought her to a Franciscan church. This woman
told her that in time she would become first a sister
of St. Joseph in France, then a Carmelite in France
and in India, and finally that she would found a
Carmelite monastery in Bethlehem.

For several years Mariam treasured these promises
in her heart while working as a maid. Her joyful
goodness made her deeply loved in all the houses
where she lived. Nonetheless, she was twice accused
of theft and once thrown into prison until the real
thief was found. At one of these houses, Mariam met
a French woman who took her back to France where
she became a sister of St. Joseph.

She was beloved for her joy, simplicity, and affec-
tionateness. But when Mariam began to receive the
first signs of the stigmata, her superiors thought it
better that she enter the Carmel of Pau where she
could enjoy greater seclusion.

As a Carmelite she insisted on taking charge of
the most menial of tasks. Her favorite name for her-

self was not "the little flower," but "the little nothing." In the very midst of chores, Mariam would be taken up in ecstasies. She would be found in the laundry rapt in a trance and singing spiritual songs. What was most delightful was the way she would levitate, flying in the air to the top of the trees, balancing on thin branches as if she were a bird.[3] She would also dictate supernatural poetry of sweet lyrical beauty.

But all was not idyllic. The phenomena of the stigmata continued and with them seasons of what seemed like hell itself.[4] During times of severe demonic temptation, Mariam would become angry and disobedient to the rule. She was deeply ashamed of these incidents, but her spiritual directors assured her that these attacks were allowed by God to make her even more like Jesus who endured temptation. She would conquer by means of the cross.[5] Other charisms included ecstatic trances, transpiercing of the heart, apparitions, bilocation, and angelic possession. During her ecstasies the work Mariam had at hand would be accomplished in some miraculous manner.

Here are a few accounts of such supernatural happenings:

At Pau, July 29, 1873, after reaching her place in the refectory, she raised a glass of water to her lips. She immediately went into an ecstasy, and seemed to be listening to a concert. Suddenly she began to sing, improvising, as was her habit, both words and music. With one hand she beat time, with the other, she held the glass without spilling the water, notwithstanding the rhythm she kept with her body. A simple word of the prioress brought the ecstatic back to earthly reality.... Let us listen to the mistress of novices: "one cannot imagine how interesting she was, with her radiant face, her shining eyes that seemed fixed on the heavenly vision that was enrapturing her. She smiled, she trembled with joy, she sang."[6]

At Pau, on Good Friday April 10, 1868, the stigmatist was truly on the cross; all her wounds reopened and the blood flowed from her heart as well. We cannot conceive the intensity of the suffering she experienced. First she felt her legs pulled one after the other; and the same with her arms; then she felt the nails being driven in.... Later, the heart bled as usual, and immediately after that, the wounds began to heal.[7]

In 1876 Sister Josephine was in residence on the island of Cyprus, when she fell gravely ill, consumed by fever. Expecting her death at any moment, the superior from time to time put a mirror to her lips to assure herself that she was still breathing. One night, about eleven o'clock, a religious entered the dying nun's cell. The visitor was elevated above the ground, her arms in the form of a cross, and a bright light enveloped her, illuminating the whole room. It was Sister Mary of Jesus Crucified [Mariam's name in Carmel].... But the sick nun had never met her. "I had never seen her, but I knew it was she, and I knew that she was speaking with the good God; I was wide awake. I called her by name and she answered me. I said to her: 'Mary, ask the good God if I am going to die.' She spoke to our Lord, and after a few seconds, said to me: 'No, you will not die young, you have much good to accomplish.'" [At this time Mariam was in the Carmel at Nazareth. The sick nun recovered and later met Mariam in the Holy Land and confirmed the experience.][8]

Although Mariam remained illiterate, she became world-famous because of the dictation to others of her prophetic words. These were so compelling that the letters sent on her behalf to bishops and popes resulted in many initiatives including the founding of Carmels in India, Bethlehem, and Nazareth. Mariam died at age thirty-three and was beatified in 1983.

In the case of mystics such as Blessed Mariam we cannot speak of some special spiritual teaching. Nonetheless, we can speak of certain landmarks on her journey. These are listed by her biographer as these: the consciousness of her misery and powerlessness; the ardent pursuit of the will of God; and the primacy of a love that stimulates the desire for heaven as the fullness of love.[9]

Many Christians like to fantasize that with more advantages in life such as a prominent family, wealth, certain educational degrees, or fewer children to take care of, they could be so much more effective in their apostolates. The life of the mystic

Mariam illustrates instead the truth of the beatitudes. Persecuted to death in her youth yet with a pure heart, she seems to have attracted the Virgin Mary and the Holy Spirit to shower graces upon her. All who knew her and the church as a whole are able to share the happy results.

NATURAL ANALOGIES

Many of the mystics loved to draw analogies between nature and grace. Mariam was able to find comfort in such comparisons even under the stress of diabolical persecution.

You [the devil] tempt me against faith?... But I have God with me; I fear nothing. You tell me there is no God? I go to the garden and contemplate creation; I see the little trees becoming full-grown; the sight increases my faith. You tempt me against the Church? I go to the garden again; I find a fruit and I open it; I look at this open fruit and I see the seed in the fruit. I go into a church, I open the tabernacle and I find the Eucharist. You tempt me against charity? I go down to the garden; I consider the animals, I see the lambs, the chicks, I see them all together, united among themselves. You tempt me against confession: I do not consider the man; I confess to Jesus.[10]

In the case of her spiritual poetry or songs, admirers point to the Semitic tonality of psalm-like utterances such as these:

To what shall I liken me?
To little birds in their nest.
If the father and mother do not bring them food,

they die of hunger. Thus is my soul without You, Lord; it does not have its nourishment, it cannot live!

To what shall I liken me?
To the little grain of wheat cast into the earth. If the dew falls not, if the sun does not warm it, the grain molds.
But if You give your dew and your sun, the little grain will be refreshed and warmed; it will take root and will produce a beautiful plant with many grains.

To what shall I liken me, Lord?
To a rose that is cut and left to dry up in the hand. It loses its perfume; but if it remains on the rosebush, it is always fresh and beautiful and keeps all its perfume.

Keep me, Lord, to give me life in You.

To what shall I liken you, Lord?
To the dove that feeds its little ones, to a tender mother who nourishes her little babe.[11]

My enraptured spirit contemplates all Your works.
    Who can speak of Thee, O God so great!
    O Omnipotent One, (it is) my ravished soul!
A nothing, a bit of dust says to You: Come to me.
    Who can say that an Omnipotent One takes notice!
One glance! You who look at me, come to me.
    You alone, my God, my all.
I see Thee, goodness supreme: Thy glance is maternal.
Come quickly, O Sun of justice, arise!
My soul is consumed, I languish while waiting,
    Come quickly!

My soul, fly with wings of the dove to my God:
   He is my All.
Thy glance consoles me, my soul is thrilled.
The nothing, the dust trembles
   in the presence of a God so great.
He has visited His field: fly away O my soul!
My soul sees Thee in the cloud,
   it can no longer remain here below.
Thy glance is enough to draw the nothing from this
      earth.
God is splendid in His power.
   Let all things praise Him, praise Him!
My soul is foolish, it can bear no more, take it!
   Who has God, possesses all things.[12]

Hail, hail, Tree of life,
   that gives us the fruit of life!
From the center of this earth
   my heart repines, my heart sighs out.
Oh! Who will give me wings
   to fly to my Beloved!

Hail, hail, Tree of life,
   that gives us the fruit of life!
I see on thy leaves these words are written:
   have no fear of anything!
Thy verdure says: Have hope.
Thy branches tell me: Charity.
And Thy shade: Humility.

Hail, hail, Tree of life;
   In Thee I find the fruit of life.
From the center of this earth,

my heart repines, my heart is longing.
Oh! Who will give me wings
   to fly to my Beloved!

Hail, hail, blessed Tree;
   Thou bearest the fruit of life.
Under Thy shade, I wish to sigh
   at thy feet, I wish to die.[13]

On returning to her beloved Carmel of Pau after her stay in India: Lord, I am like the little chick that the kite bird has caught; it has pricked it on the head, it has almost crushed it; but the poor little thing has escaped to safety under its mother's wing. I too have been in anguish, sadness, sorrow. My bones were dislocated; the marrow of my bones was embittered within me, my flesh was bruised. I turn my gaze toward my Father, and He looked at me, and this glance healed me. The marrow of my bones, which was embittered, has become sweet as sugar; my bones were made as strong as if I were fifteen years old.... I ran to my Father and my King. And my King also came to me. And I was with thee like the little chick under its mother's wing. I looked at my enemies through the wing feathers of my Father and my King, without fearing anything; I was in safety.[14]

SUFFERING AND UNION

Perhaps you are one who envies the stigmatists their bodily resemblance to Jesus Christ in his passion. You might think of all your natural bodily infirmities as your way of participating in his sufferings.

Lord, my land is dry and parched:
   send your dew.
My flesh is falling off in rottenness,
   my feet can no longer support me,
   nor my hands move.

My nerves are all on edge;
   my bones are wasted away,
   the marrow of my bones is like rotten smoke.
The hairs of my head are stiff,
   all standing straight up
   and they prick me like needles.
My ears are closed
   and so dull I cannot hear.
My eyes are on fire,
   they no longer see the light.
My nose is all pinched;
My tongue cleaves to my palate
   and can no longer utter a word
   to cry to You.
My teeth are so locked
   the air can no longer pass through
   and I am going to die.
My lips are so tight closed
   that I can no longer move them
   to call You to my aid.
Lord, send Your dew upon this sterile earth,
   and it will return to life.

At the feet of Mary, my mother dear,
   I came back to life.
O all you who suffer, come to Mary,

at the feet of Mary I came back to life.
O you who work in this monastery,
   Mary counts your steps and your labors.
   Tell yourselves:
   at the feet of Mary, I came back to life.
You who dwell in this monastery,
   detach yourselves from the things of earth.
Your salvation and your life are at the feet of Mary.
I dwell in the heart of my mother,
   there I find my Beloved.
Am I then an orphan? In the bosom of Mary
   I have found life.
Do not say I am an orphan:
   I have Mary for Mother and God for Father.
The serpent, the dragon wished to catch me
   and take my life;
   but at the feet of Mary, I recovered my life.
Mary called me, and, in this monastery,
   will I remain forever.
   At the feet of Mary
   I came to life again.[15]

During a forty-day assault by Satan, she prayed:
Always more suffering for you, Jesus!
I weep, O Jesus, for not suffering enough for you.
I unite myself to Jesus when He was carrying His
cross in the streets of Jerusalem. May You be blessed,
my God.
I unite my voice with that of Jesus in the garden of
olives. May You be blessed, my God.
I unite my sufferings to those of Jesus betrayed by
Judas. May You be blessed, my God....

I desire to suffer, to be immolated, crushed, roasted, until the end of the world, for the triumph of the Church. My God, may You be blessed!...

Lord, I deserve rather to be thrust down, to the bottom. Forgive me, forgive me!

Ask Jesus to deliver me from the interior joys that I experience. They are so great that I do not feel any suffering.

Mary, my mother, come to my help! Everyone cry out with me: Jesus, wake up!

Lord, I accept all that You will.

Love, O love, you are not known![16]

PRAYERS OF PRAISE

Most delightful of Mariam Baouardy's prayers are those dedicated to praise. Let this motif never be absent from our own dialogue with the Creator.

The whole world is asleep, and God so full of goodness, so great, so worthy of all praise, no one is thinking of Him! See, nature praises Him, and man... who ought to praise Him, sleeps! Let us go, let us go and wake up the universe... and sing His praises.[17]

I invited the whole earth, to bless Thee, to serve Thee.

Forever and always, never to end! With Thy love my heart made one.

I invited the entire sea, to bless Thee, to serve Thee.

Forever and always, never to end!

I called them, invited them, little birds of the air, to bless Thee, to serve Thee.

Forever and always, never to end!
I called, I invited, the star of the morn. Forever and
   always, never to end!

My Beloved, yes I hear Him, He is very near, Go for-
   ward! Forever and ever and always, never to end!
Open, O curtain that hides Him, I want to see Him,
   my Beloved, to adore and to love.
Forever and always, never to end! With His love my
   heart made one.
I called him, invited ungrateful man, to bless Thee,
   to serve Thee, to praise and to love Thee, Forever
   and always, never to end.[18]

My enraptured spirit contemplates all your works.
Who can speak of You, O God so great!
Omnipotent One, my soul is carried away!
His wonderful beauty delights my soul.
Who can tell what the Almighty looks upon?
One look!
You who gaze at me, come to me, a little nothing.
I cannot remain here on earth, my soul longing.
Call me close to You, awaken me.
You alone, my God, my All.
The heavens, the earth, the sun rejoice at your
   Name so great.
I see You, supreme goodness: your gaze is maternal.
My Father, my Mother, it is in You that I sleep,
It is in You that I breathe. Awaken!
My soul is mad with yearning, it can do no more,
   take it.
When will we see Him forever world without end![19]

16

Concepción Cabrera de Armida (Conchita)
(1862–1937)

There are priceless moments during which I feel a strange phenomenon—as it were a joy at the heart of suffering.... That seemed incredible to me who had turned my back on it, tried to avoid it countless times despite the attraction God had given me toward hidden suffering.... When the soul is engulfed in pain, at these very moments, almost of despair, there comes a gentle breeze, changing parching arid suffering into a pleasant freshness, without other desire than to please the Beloved, without dreaming any more about the pleasure of future goods. No, all this becomes or appears secondary in comparison with the joy of pleasing Him.[1]

✠ ✠ ✠

C AN GRANDMOTHERS BE MYSTICS? "And why not?" this grandmother and author of a book called *Prayers of the Women Mystics* would reply! Surely one of the most lovable contemplative-actives of our times is Concepción Cabrera de Armida: a Mexican wife, mother, grandmother, and mystic who is slated for beatification in the near future.

Concepción Cabrera de Armida, called by all Conchita, was born in 1862 in San Luis Potosí, Mexico. Raised on the family ranch, this lovely and lively girl spent lots of time horseback riding, laughing, playing the piano, and singing. Her youth was more carefree because the Catholic schools were being closed as persecution of the church by anti-Catholics gained ascendancy.

Conchita's family was very devout. Her mother brought up the twelve children in a holy manner and her father presided over the rosary that was said every day by the whole family and all the farm workers.

So delightful was Conchita that she could count twenty-two suitors by the time she finally settled on her beloved Pancho, chosen because he was the most pious of the lot. On her wedding day, Conchita asked but two promises of her spouse: no matter how many children we have, will you be sure that I can go to daily Mass? And will you never be jealous? Pancho faithfully kept the first promise even when they had nine children.

Needless to say, Conchita's request to commune daily with the Lord did not come out of the childish fun and games that characterized her outward life as a girl. Hidden within was a deep desire not only for prayer but for penance. Her burning love for Christ, desire to save souls, and special need to do penance for the sanctification of priests grew steadily in the early years of her marriage. Her desire culminated in this incident:

By dint of many a plea, I got my director's permission to engrave the initials (J.H.S.) on the feast of the Holy Name of Jesus, January 14, 1894.... I cut on my bosom in large letters: J.H.S. No sooner had I done this than I felt a supernatural force which threw me, face down, on the floor, my eyes filled with tears and a burning flame within my heart. Vehemently and zealously I then asked the Lord for the salvation of souls: "Jesus, Savior of souls, save them, save them!"... The ardor of my soul far surpassed the burning sensation of my body and I experienced an ineffable joy on feeling I belonged wholly to Jesus, just as a branded animal to its owner.[2]

This rich interior life was not something distinct from or opposed to her family life. In those days many husbands liked to spend their evenings with other men rather than with their wives and children. Conchita had a remedy: "I had accustomed my husband, an excellent man, to come home early and find everything there without having to seek elsewhere certain diversions. I surrounded him with a multitude of attentions. When his birthday came, I gave him eighteen or twenty presents.... He helped me put the children to bed and lull them to sleep. His home and his children, there was all his happiness."[3]

Conchita's biographer writes about his interviews with her children: "Mama always smiled." When he told them "Your mama was a great saint and a great mystic," they straightaway replied, "Saint or mystic, we do not know, but mother, the greatest mother that ever lived!"[4]

Two family deaths were to deepen Conchita's sense of the transitory nature of this earth and the permanence of eternal happiness. The first was the death of her son Carlos at age six, over whom she grieved much. It was a liberating moment when Conchita was finally willing to give away a treasured garment of her beloved little son to a poor boy of the neighborhood.

The second death was just as painful. After sixteen years of marriage, her beloved Pancho died. Conchita grieved horrendously as she anticipated the loss of this good man:

This sword pierced my soul, without any assuagement, without any consolation. This very night, the Lord presented to me the chalice and made me drink of it drop by drop to the dregs. During these days, I visited the Tabernacle for sustenance and strength. Oh! If I had not been sustained by Him, then through my great weakness, I would have succumbed.... What a model husband! What a model father! What an upright man! What finesse, what delicacy in his relations with me, so respectful in all his actions, so Christian in all his thoughts, so honest, so perfect in everything he did!... Oh! how ephemeral is life! How short our existence! How near to each other are the present and the past! What do we do when this time is not employed for God alone?[5]

Life became very difficult for the widow with so many small children yet to raise. But it was at this time that Conchita met the holy priest, Fr. Felix Rougier, who was to become with her co-founder of the many apostolates called The Works of the Cross. These now include the Missionaries of the Holy Spirit, an order of priests; the Sisters of the Cross, enclosed contemplatives; an order to catechetical sisters; an alliance for lay people offering their sufferings for the Church; and an Apostolic League for bishops and priests. In connection with the founding of these groups, Conchita made several trips to Rome.

Although there were many years free from obligatory family duties when she could have lived in the contemplative convent, God instead led Conchita to remain in the world. Here she offered her exterior and interior sufferings for the intentions of the apostolates.

At her death in 1937, this saintly woman left behind not only her children, grandchildren, and her foundations but also large volumes of her diaries and other shorter works that are gradually being translated into other languages. A book of letters to her children is of particular help to other mothers. Many Catholics make use of her booklet *Before the Altar*[6] for Eucharistic adoration. The prayers which I have used are all drawn from this booklet.

What is the essence of the spiritual teaching of Conchita? The love of Christ for the soul is of a tenderness and sublimity that should make all Christians open themselves to interior prayer, seeking here what they seek in vain in lesser loves. Sufferings of daily life should not be seen as merely unavoidable burdens, but as treasures that can be offered for the evangelization of peoples and the sanctification of those who only partially believe.

The mystical spirituality of Conchita provides us with a possible pathway to perpetual union with God. We can experience this oneness not only in action but also in bringing the deepest yearnings of our souls into unity with the God of compassionate love.

Consider how badly we feel when those we love hide the movements of their hearts from us, refusing to open themselves to the love we want to give in comfort. Our pain offers but a glimpse of the pain of the Divine Lover—so often shut out when we get sucked into a downward spiral of depression and despair. May Conchita's experience give us courage once more to be vulnerable with the only person who has never betrayed us.

JESUS ALONE

Many serious Christians think of Jesus as dwelling in the center of their hearts, but rarely as the only one who can give them the deepest peace and joy. We know that we are not thinking of Jesus alone whenever we feel this peace pushed out of place by desires and frustrations about other loves. We do need human love, but we should come to others with tenderness rather than with desperate thirst.

Jesus, God and Spouse of my soul! You alone, you alone... when shall I end by understanding it? I shall always find You disposed, O my Jesus, to listen to me, day, night, *always*!

If I cling to human affection I shall find nothing but illusion and disappointment!... Do You in mercy tear me away from all that is not Yourself.... Let me be forgotten and forsaken, for *Thy mercy's sake*, so that all that is earthly can be removed from my heart. Do this for the good of my soul, which is so inclined to attach itself to creatures and which, nevertheless, only desires to belong to You, my Jesus....

You alone... shall console me in my sorrows, dry my tears, receive my last kiss, and be my companion at the hour of my death, when all others shall forsake me. And last of all, Your picture, this adored image on the Cross, which I have kissed during life shall be the silent witness of my total destruction in the grave.

This is why *You alone, O my Jesus!* You alone, shall ever be my only love.[7]

O Jesus! Love of my soul, You shall always remain to me, even though I should lose all else: my father, and my mother, my family, my director, my friends. ... Yes, You shall remain, for you do not die, You change not and the fire of Your Heart is as ardent as ever!

What matters to me therefore, the long distance which separates me from those I love, if He who keeps hidden in His Heart all the tenderness of the earth is to be found at my side?...

I remember those who have gone before me into Eternity, and my eyes are turned toward You, O

Saviour of my soul, because it is *there* that I come across them. It is there that they wait for me, bathed in the brightness of Your pure and holy light....

That is why I place all my happiness in possessing You, in having You to be mine... in loving You passionately, madly, with all the tenderness of all loving hearts; with all the heart beatings of pure souls....

What an unspeakable consolation to keep one's eyes fixed on Your Divine Heart, so good, so loving; and to hear you saying in my inmost soul: "My child, give Me your heart."[8]

Yes, Jesus, I am poor and have the voluntary poverty which rejoices in possessing nothing and returning everything to You.

I long for actual poverty... because I love You and wish to resemble You, O Jesus of my soul!...

I wish to be poor in honor.... I wish to be poor in man's esteem and friendship....

I wish to leave empty the place I occupy in other hearts, that you Yourself may occupy it.

Oh, what a precious exchange, what a truly heavenly thing; You reigning in the souls of others, and I, like a slave, at everybody's feet in the dust.... O my King.... give me the grace to deprive myself voluntarily of *all that is pleasing to my nature,* and at the same time to abandon myself entirely into Your hands.[9]

I have no other love but You, my supreme Good, my Life, my heaven, my only desire; and all other loves, great but with human limitations, although pure and legitimate in their origin, because sanctified by contact with You, all these loves are also Yours, my Jesus.[10]

THE NEED FOR MERCY

At certain times in the spiritual life, we can have the illusion that we have arrived at a high plateau and that we more or less deserve eternal rewards. The sensitivity that comes with further graces, however, soon shows us how unloving our lives really are. With that realization comes a deep call not for justice but for mercy.

Oh yes, Jesus, *my Life!* The end of my day is approaching and I wish to keep quite close to You, for the cold chills me, if I withdraw from You ever so little. In order to be happy and at peace, I need the gentle warmth of Your Heart, of Your words, of Your looks!...

I have wasted the better part of my life in vanities, in imaginations, in vain pleasures and in foolish illusions.... There are immense voids in my life: I have not always done my duty to my neighbor, or to the members of my family.... Instead of seeking God, I have sought myself. I have desired comforts, I have been vainglorious and obstinate in defending my own opinion. I have taken pleasure in worldly friendships, and have sought myself even in my private devotions.... What excuses, what idleness, selfishness, sensuality and sluggishness in the service of God....

What touchiness, cowardice and uncharitableness! O my Jesus, it makes me tremble when I consider that it *is the end of the day*, that night is coming on, and that my heart, alas! remains full of vices, stains and iniquities!...

Where are the humility, the patience, the obedience, the gentleness, the costly victories?... Where are to be found the unlimited charity... the hunger for solitude... in all of which I should have placed my happiness?...

O my Jesus! and this is why I suffer, because my hands are empty, and the Bridegroom will soon be here and I shall have neither the oil of virtues nor the ardent flame of love, to offer Him![11]

I look and look, and turn to look again at the consecrated Host; its whiteness dazzles me; its brilliant rays wound my soul to its utmost depths by revealing to me all its defects and deformities.

Who can wish himself pure in the presence of Purity itself? Who is without spot before the spotlessness of Jesus?

Who can think himself humble in the presence of Him who is hidden under the form of bread?...

Who will believe himself innocent before the immaculate Lamb?...

Oh, my Lord! In Your presence, I ought to feel nought but shame, and a deep sense of my utter worthlessness; but I also feel great love for You, a burning love, which in uniting me to You, consumes all the vileness of my poor heart; a love which purifies and transforms me, and takes me far away from this earth, to the purest of Hosts, the very abode of Love.[12]

"Go and sin no more." This is what Jesus says to me every time I go to confession.... These words of our Lord touch me to the quick. How delicate is the heart of Jesus, such love and such tenderness could proceed only from God!

And how do I respond to His wonderful goodness? What are the fruits derived from my confessions?

Do I not always come back with the same sins, the same defects, the same imperfections?

Can I truly say that since I heard those sweet words of Jesus, I have not fallen again into sin?

Have I preserved that peace of soul which *a tranquil* conscience alone can give, or have I allowed it to be taken from me in a thousand different ways?...

How often when kneeling at the feet of the priest, have I not sought rather to obtain consolation than to repent and weep over my sins? Alas, how often also, in that holy place have I not sought myself! How often have I not feared to lay bare all my weaknesses!

How often have I not excused my imperfections, spoken ill of others, and sought to please my confessor without giving a thought to that contrition and voluntary humiliation, which should always accompany my confession!...

Pardon me, Lord, pardon me for my want of delicacy to You and for my exceeding great pride, which manifests itself even in the most sacred things.[13]

FEELINGS OF ABANDONMENT

It can help us to realize that even the saints who were the closest to God and the most pure of heart still often felt desolate and abandoned by God.

Why, O Jesus! my Own, my Life, my All, do you hide Yourself from me?...

Why does that Heart, whose fiery flames I have felt so often, which has beaten against my heart, which has made mine a thousand times leap for joy, why does it appear today to be unconscious of my tears and of my sufferings?...

Why is it that, living as I do beneath the burning rays of my Eucharistic Sun, everything around me is ice, indifference and pain?

Why, Love of my loves, my Heaven, my Life, Heart of my soul, why leave my soul to be immersed and lose itself in an ocean of suffering?

Is it for my sins or for those of others? Is it to punish me? Is it out of love to purify me? O my Beloved, ... do not forsake me: have Pity on me, for it is death to me, to be without Him who is my Life!

My days are nights, my nights are purgatory, my mind is hell.... The hours are a continual martyrdom without Him who is my Light, my very breath, my heart and my Heaven!

O Jesus, Jesus, what shall I do to find You? Ah, I know. *Not to find myself*, who am the cause of my own unhappiness. I must disappear, diminish, descend, and be reduced to nothing, in order that You must grow, and reign, and occupy in my heart the place which I have prepared for You!... You must be *All* in the heart of Your poor child.[14]

What the martyrs suffered is as nothing, compared to the anguish endured by a soul that possesses God and does not feel His presence.

What torture can be compared with that felt by a soul which is possessed of God and is yet apparently abandoned by Him!... How bitter the sorrows unknown to the world and only understood by those who love You!

I know by faith that You are with me, but I do not see You, I do not perceive You, I do not touch You; and darkness and temptations, abandonment and all kinds of bitterness paralyze my soul....

This is called the martyrdom of love, more trying and more painful than all the different kinds of martyrdom put together....

It seems to me that a mountain of ice lies between us, although Your heart could melt in an instant the eternal snows; a thousand clouds surround me and bar the way and prevent me from approaching that Treasure.... A thousand veils envelop me nor can I tear them asunder in order to contemplate You....

Oh Jesus, my heaven, when will daylight come to me!

Have you known the martyrdom, my beloved Mother, of possessing God and not feeling His presence? Ah, yes, I doubt it not for a moment, since You are the Queen of Martyrs, and you have suffered all that can be suffered. Help me to bear this heavy Cross with love and patience![15]

I come to You today, bathed in tears, with my heart shedding its blood drop by drop, and my soul plunged in an ocean of bitterness.

But what better preparation could I have to contemplate and understand You as a Victim in this most adorable sacrament? Were You not immersed Yourself, O my Master! in an ocean of sufferings... of sorrows... of weariness ... and of fear... and all that Your Sacred humanity, miraculously sustained by the Divinity itself, was capable of suffering?

And, therefore, O my Jesus, the more bitter, the more profound, the more vast and the more agitated, becomes this ocean of sorrows in which I am plunged, the more I will rejoice, because that way I shall the more resemble You....[16]

UNION WITH CHRIST IN THE EUCHARIST

Of the women mystics described in this book, Conchita is one of those most devoted to the Eucharist. Our lives are much more agitated in some ways than those of Conchita. In these busy times, more and more Catholics are discovering the peace to be found in quiet adoration early in the morning, in the evening, and even at night. Some faithful parishioners are getting permission to have a key so that they can come to visit Jesus even when the church is locked.

You are my Love, O my Jesus in the Holy Eucharist. My first thought on waking is of You, beloved of my soul, and my last before closing my eyes in sleep is of that consecrated Host, with an ardent longing for the dawn of another day when I can approach You and receive You again in the Holy Communion....

I think of You before dawn... even before the birds have begun to salute You with their morning song. I think of You in the midday heat; and when the shades of night surround me the remembrance of You and of Your love afford me the brightest of lights.

O Jesus of the Eucharist! O consecrated Host! O envied Monstrance! O blessed Ciborium, beloved of my heart! The Tabernacle is my Treasure, and, far or near, my eyes never lose sight of it, for it contains the God of Love.[17]

O my child, son of the Cross and of My Heart, your father and mother may fail you, but *I* will never abandon you!

Even at my death, I did not leave my children orphans, for, day and night, they can find me upon their altars.

With the tenderness, and gentleness of a thousand mothers, the Last Supper came to sweeten the bitterness of Calvary; for I knew that in the Holy Eucharist you would ever have with you a father and a mother, and would never be alone while on earth....

I wished, My beloved child, that My body, which was crushed under the burden of the cross, and My blood, which was shed for all mankind, should be your consolation and joy within this Sacrament.... The thought that you would be happy in the possession of the Holy Eucharist, increased my strength during My passion, and lessened My fear....

It was this thought that caused Me to sing joyfully the song of thanksgiving as I walked with my Apostles to the Garden of Olives.... When My body was being cruelly scourged... and when My blood was pouring on the ground, I rejoiced, My dearly beloved son, I rejoiced at being ground like wheat in the mill and pressed like grapes in the wine-press, thus making Myself the bread and the wine with which to nourish you at the Eucharistic banquet.

Before death had taken Me away from men, I had disposed and arranged to multiply my life upon their altars....

O Jesus, O my beloved Jesus! O Jesus hidden here beneath these Sacramental veils! Grant that at every moment of my life I may return to You gratitude and love, in return for Your great love for me![18]

Can the soul explain what a consecrated Host is, what she feels on seeing It and when approaching It, and what is the sensation produced by Divine contact with It in Holy Communion?

Who can see You, O Sacred Host, without being moved? Who is not attracted by Your Divine charms? Who on feeling Your burning rays does not feel Your warmth, and drink of the fountain of life?

Who does not feel his faith, his hope and his love augment in the presence of Your incomprehensible abasement?...

I carry Your image, O Sacred Host, engraved in my memory, but far more in my heart; my looks and my thoughts, piercing brick walls, silk, the precious metals and even the appearance of bread which hides You, my Jesus....[19]

17

Blessed Elizabeth of the Trinity
(1880–1906)

"A Praise of Glory" is a soul of silence that remains like a lyre under the mysterious touch of the Holy Spirit so that He may draw from it divine harmonies; it knows that suffering is a string that produces still more beautiful sounds; so it loves to see this string on its instrument that it may more delightfully move the heart of God.[1]

⌗ ⌗ ⌗

"A PRAISE OF GLORY" is Elizabeth's name for herself. The influence of this mystic on contemporary contemplatives is growing. Her delicate and exalted spirituality opens new vistas of insight.[2]

Elizabeth Catez was born in 1880 to a French military family. Shortly after her birth they moved to the city of Dijon. Although considered to be a little devil as a tot and capable of terrible rages as a young girl, Elizabeth's fiery qualities were gradually channeled by breeding and grace. By young adulthood she would be described by all who knew her as enchanting, vivacious, and tender.

Filled with a love for the beauty and grandeur of nature, Elizabeth radiates a cosmic expansiveness in all that she writes about God and prayer. At a time when many young girls studied piano in a dilettantish sort of way, she became an accomplished pianist and prize winner. Musical analogies enliven her later spiritual writings. The following excerpt highlights her concept of harmony in all—the hallmark of Elizabeth's conception of interior peace.

A soul that debates with its self, that is taken up with its feelings, and pursues useless thoughts and desires, scatters its forces, for it is not wholly directed toward God. Its lyre does not vibrate in unison and when the Master plays it, He cannot draw from it divine harmonies, for it is still too human and discordant. The soul that still keeps something for itself in its "inner kingdom," whose powers are not "enclosed" in God, cannot be a perfect praise of glory; it is not fit to sing uninterruptedly this "canticum magnum" of which St. Paul speaks since unity does not reign in it. Instead of persevering in praise through everything in simplicity, it must continually adjust the strings of its instrument which are all a little out of tune.[3]

This saint's youthful piety was characterized by intense inner listening, which began with her First Holy Communion. Elizabeth's prayer life continually deepened. When fourteen years old, she felt impelled by the Holy Spirit to consecrate her life to Jesus in a vow of perpetual virginity.

When Elizabeth's now widowed mother tried to interest her daughter in courtship, the young woman could not comply. Although she describes herself as coquettish and elegant, her real desire was to live for Jesus alone as a Carmelite. One of her potential suitors remarked to another admirer of Elizabeth: "No, she is not for us."

At the Carmel of Dijon, right next to the family dwelling, she was given the name Elizabeth of the Trinity because she had a special sense of the presence of the three persons of the Trinity indwelling her soul. She died only six years after her entry into the convent and was beloved by all who knew her.

Elizabeth was full of love and carried on a lively correspondence with relatives and friends she knew before her profession. One of the ways her tenderness expressed itself in the convent was by her graced intuition about what truth each sister most needed to hear. A touching example comes in this letter to her mother superior to be opened after Elizabeth's death:

> "You are uncommonly loved," loved by that love of preference that the Master had here below for some and which brought them so far. He does not say to you as to Peter: "Do you love Me more than these?" Mother, listen to what He tells you: "*Let* yourself be loved more than these! That is,

without fearing that any obstacle will be a hindrance to it, for I am free to pour out My love on whom I wish! '*Let* yourself be loved more than these' is your vocation. It is in being faithful to it that you will make Me happy for you will magnify the power of My love. This love can rebuild what you have destroyed. Let yourself be loved more than these."[4]

About her impending death, Elizabeth wrote:

David sang: "My soul falls down in a faint for the courts of the Lord." I think that this should be the attitude of every soul that enters into its interior courts to contemplate its God and to come into closest contact with Him: it "falls down in a faint" in a divine swoon before this all-powerful Love, this infinite Majesty who dwells within it! It is not life that abandons the soul, but rather the soul that scorns this natural life and withdraws from it.... For it feels that this life is not worthy of His rich essence so it dies and flows into its God.[5]

Concerning how she would spend her eternity, and if, like "Little Thérèse," she would come down to earth for the good of souls, she replied: "Oh! no, indeed, as soon as I reach the threshold of Paradise, I will rush like a little rocket into the bosom of 'my Three'; a Praise of Glory can have no other place for eternity and I will plunge ever deeper into it...." Then, after a little pause, with her eyes closed and her hands joined, she added: "However, if God grants my request, I think that in Heaven my mission will be to draw souls into *interior recollection.*"[6]

The writings of Elizabeth of the Trinity were published after her death, mostly in the form of letters and short spiritual treatises. They are studded with scriptural reflections and with the spirit of praise, for she considered her vocation to be offering continual praise for the glory of God.

In his introduction to her collected works, Conrad De Meester writes:

It seems to us that Elizabeth of the Trinity... presents a prophetic aspect by the gentleness and flexibility with which she lived.... There is nothing harsh, hard, or irritating about her—apart from a few short periods of transition, for she, too, must have had to struggle. In her silence there is a freedom which she had already acquired as a young lay person. Her neighbor does not feel rejected, but, on the contrary, drawn to her Mystery. We detect in her an exceptional combination of the mystical and the human, of attention to God and a deep sense of friendship....

Elizabeth also surpasses the current spirituality of her day by *her enthusiastic and loving approach to the Trinity.* She is overcome with wonder before God who, however exalted and immense he may be, is not alone in his majesty but is a Community of Love: Three in a union which surpasses all understanding—creating man and inviting him to live and act in him who is Love. For her the holiness of God radiates an infinite love! To draw near him is to be freed from the evil that is in us, to be enkindled with the fire of the Spirit.[7]

De Meester also points out that Elizabeth is part of the current movement in spirituality of discovering "Scripture as the charter of Christian life."[8] Even her name, "Praise of Glory," is taken from the Word of God: "We have been predestined by the decree of Him who works all things according to the counsel of His will, so that we may be *the praise of His glory*" (cf. Ephesians 1:11-12).

Sometimes our prayer life becomes a little cluttered. We may have undertaken certain daily prayers such as the Liturgy of the Hours and the rosary, in addition to meditation on Scripture and petitions for particular intentions. We can begin to think of these as the obligatory prayers and the time of quiet opening to God in silence as the optional part—to be squeezed in only if we are not too busy that day. The prayers of Blessed Elizabeth of the Trinity counsel us to give more weight to the longing of our hearts for solitude and silent communion with God as the climax of our prayer.

THE PRAYERS OF BLESSED ELIZABETH OF THE TRINITY

Perhaps because of the musical quality of her interior life, Elizabeth's prayers do not lend themselves to division into categories. Rather, they form one song, a medley of themes concerning the Trinity: indwelling, praise, surrender. The has become one of those most often found in Catholic prayer books:

O my God, Trinity Whom I adore
help me to forget myself entirely
that I may be established in You
as still and as peaceful
as if my soul were already in eternity.

May nothing trouble my peace
or make me leave You,
O my Unchanging One,
but may each minute
carry me further
into the depths of Your Mystery.

Give peace to my soul,
make it Your heaven,
Your beloved dwelling
and Your resting place.

May I never leave You there alone
but be wholly present,
my faith wholly vigilant,
wholly adoring,
and wholly surrendered to Your creative Action.

O my beloved Christ,
crucified by love,
I wish to be a bride for Your heart;
I wish to cover You with glory;
I wish to love You…
even unto death!

But I feel my weakness,
and I ask You to "clothe me with Yourself,"
to identify my soul with all the movements of Your
    Soul,
to overwhelm me,
to possess me,
to substitute Yourself for me
that my life may be but a radiance of Your Life.

Come into me as Adorer,
as Restorer,
as Savior.
O Eternal Word, Word of my God,
I want to spend my life in listening to You,
to become wholly teachable
that I may learn all from You.
Then, through all nights, all voids, all helplessness,
I want to gaze on you always and remain in Your
    great light.

O my beloved Star,
so fascinate me
that I may not withdraw from Your radiance.

O consuming Fire,
Spirit of Love,
"come upon me,"
and create in my soul a kind of incarnation of the
    Word:
that I may be another humanity for Him
in which He can renew His whole Mystery.

And You, O Father,
bend lovingly over Your poor little creature,
"cover her with Your shadow,"
seeing in her only
the "Beloved in whom You are well pleased."[9]

A bridal prayer written to Jesus when Elizabeth was in her teens:
Jesus, my soul desires You,
I want to be your bride soon.
With You I want to suffer—
and to find you, die.[10]

A prayer written when it seemed to her that she might not be able to enter Carmel: May my life be a continual prayer, a long act of *love. May nothing* distract me from You, neither noise nor diversions. O my Master, I would so love to live with You in silence. But what I love above all is to do Your will, and since You want me to still remain in the world, I submit with all my heart *for love of You.* I offer You the cell of my heart; may it be Your little Bethany. Come rest there; I love You so.... I would like to console You, and I offer myself to You as a victim, O my Master, for You, with You.[11]

A bridal prayer to the Holy Spirit written later:
Holy Spirit, Goodness, Supreme Beauty!
O You Whom I adore, O You Whom I love!
Consume with Your divine flames
This body and this heart and this soul!
This spouse of the Trinity
Who desires only Your will![12]

On the indwelling, this prayer is expressed in prophetic style as coming from Christ: "'Remain in Me.' It is the Word of God who gives this order, expresses this wish. Remain in Me, not for a few moments, a few hours which must pass away, but '*remain*' permanently, habitually. Remain in Me, pray in Me, adore in Me, love in Me, suffering in Me, work and act in Me. Remain in Me so that you may be able to encounter anyone or anything; penetrate further still into these depths. This is truly the 'solitude into which God wants to allure the soul that He may speak to it,' as the prophet sang."[13]

18

Raissa Maritain
(1883–1960)

You are Truth—You are Sincerity,
But each man is a liar.
May all that is within me,
Good and evil, lie and error,
What I know and do not know,
Pray, beseech, cry to You!
If I seek to know me, I lose myself in thought—
It is You alone who know my real name,
Whether I am deserving of hatred or of love.
May Your pity rescue us through grace,...
Purify, illuminate my soul,
That it [may] escape the power of nothingness.[1]

❈ ❈ ❈

ANYONE EXPLORING SPIRITUAL LIFE in the United States in the 1990s would find it difficult to understand how profoundly Catholics earlier in this century were influenced by currents coming from European sources.[2]

As a convert studying at Fordham University in the sixties, I can recall the excitement of the publication in 1963 of *Raissa's Journal*. How astounding and inspiring to eavesdrop, as it were, on the conversations between God and this French woman— famous as the wife of Jacques Maritain, one of the leading Catholic philosophers of our times.

We university Catholics all knew the unusual story of the Maritains.[3] Jacques was born in 1882 in Paris, of a liberal Protestant family. Raissa was born to a Jewish family in 1883 in Rostoff-on-the-Don, Russia, one steeped in spirituality. When Raissa was ten the family emigrated to Paris. By fourteen she began to entertain atheistic doubts—though in her heart she clung to God. Once ready for university studies, she enrolled at the Sorbonne hoping to find the absolute truth she was seeking by the study of science.

It was at the university that Raissa met Jacques. Jacques describes Raissa as vivacious, merry, empathetic, with a marvelous smile and an extraordinary light in her eyes. They fell in love. But even this enchantment could not overcome the deep despair that flowed from their general doubt about whether life had any meaning at all and their inability to believe in God. They made a vow that if they could not find a truth that made sense of the tragedy of life, they would carry out a suicide pact.

God imparted some hope of finding *the* truth to them through the lectures of Henri Bergson, the famous philosopher of creative evolution. Raissa caught a glimpse of the mystical way of embracing the truth. Living still without certainty, they married in 1904.

Through their friendship with the provocative, prophetic Catholic writer, Léon Bloy, the Maritains were opened to the grace of faith. His book *Salvation Comes from the Jews* became a bridge for the young seeker of so Jewish a background. 1906 saw the baptism of not only Raissa and Jacques but also her younger sister, Vera, who was to spend her whole life in their home as a companion and helper. Years later Raissa's father was baptized just before his death, and then much later her mother.

Rather soon the Maritains decided that they would dwell together as "brother and sister" instead of continuing their marital relations. Their decision was based not on any distaste for each other, but on a conviction that such a sacrifice would be a holy offering to God.

Such marriages are called Josephite, with reference to the union of Mary and Joseph. Church authorities are reluctant to approve Josephite marriages and do so only in exceptional cases. After all, sexual union is the seal of the sacrament of matrimony and a right of the spouses. All care must be taken to avoid situations where a husband and wife initially agree on abstinence but later regret their vow—sometimes blaming the other partner for a wrong choice or seeking satisfaction of sexual needs outside of marriage.

Whatever the reader's opinion of Josephite marriages in general, there is no doubt of the fruitfulness of the spiritual union of Raissa and Jacques. They lived with Raissa's sister in perfect harmony, Raissa helping Jacques with his writing, he supporting her vocation of prayer, and both opening heart and home to countless persons in need of deep friendship, especially artists and writers.

All Raissa's writings are permeated with her great love for Jacques. This letter written in 1936 is reflective of her gratitude for their unique marriage:

> Go on loving me like this, I need a great deal of love in order to live and I know that *I* have to live "as not loving," in St. Paul's sense, and beyond St. Paul's sense. What a terrible vocation! It is for me that God has placed your marvelous love at my side. For with whom would I have been able to live such a vocation, except with you?... What is wonderful, is that I can take this rest in your heart without in any way hindering God's action in us. God is so much with you. And you are truly my only sweetness in this world.[4]

In a journal entry typical of Raissa's desire for a most perfect purity of intention, she writes: "I must free myself of all feeling of conceit about Jacques and the performance or the success, and even the intrinsic value of his work—so that nothing matters to me *in him* and in me but the love of God, 'regarding *everything* as dung that I may win Jesus Christ and find myself in Him,' with Jacques."[5]

Important moments in their Catholic life in-

cluded becoming Benedictine Oblates, the growth
of their devotion to Mary through the de Montfort
consecration, and their discovery of St. Thomas
Aquinas. Jacques was to dedicate his work to the
propagation of the writings of St. Thomas. Raissa—
always in semi-retirement from the world because of
recurrent illness—devoted her life to contemplative
prayer.

From the moment of her baptism, Raissa felt
drawn to silent prayer. She later received permission
from her director to make contemplative prayer the
center of her day, in fact to live as a contemplative
in the world. Raissa spent the mornings in silent
prayer from the year 1916.

Her experience of infused grace was often ecstatic, but also for many years extremely painful. We
find this entry in her journal of 1916: "I was seized
by a feeling of familiarity with God, with Jesus, with
Mary.... I wept and exulted. It was as if there were a
perpetual spring of joy, of sweetness, of happy certainty welling up in me—it lasted a long while—and
the memory of it has not been effaced."[6]

In the early part of their marriage, the Maritains
were fairly isolated. This was soon to end when
Jacques' philosophical work became more and more
important to the entire Catholic intellectual world.
Raissa's prayer became a spiritual foundation for the
active works of their friends. They also sought her
sympathetic counsel concerning their personal
problems. In collaboration with Jacques she wrote
books on prayer, liturgy, and poetry. In 1940, the

Maritains fled to the United States from war-torn Europe.

What can we say about the spiritual teaching of Raissa? Roger Voillaume, Prior of the Little Brothers of Jesus, prefaces her journals by pointing to the fact that Raissa was a contemplative who lived right in the midst of the misery of the world. She thereby witnessed to the possibility of such prayer for all lay people.[7] Raissa expresses this call:

> We walk in darkness, risking bruising ourselves against a thousand obstacles. But we know that "God is Love" and trust in God as our light. I have the feeling that what is asked of us is to live in the whirlwind, without keeping back any of our substance, without keeping back anything for ourselves, neither rest nor friendships nor health nor leisure—to pray incessantly and that even without leisure—in fact to let ourselves pitch and toss in the waves of the divine will till the day when it will say: "That's enough."[8]

One of Raissa's themes addresses these times of turbulent church dispute: truth should not isolate us but rather draw us closer to others. We ought to look at the world with sympathy and understanding, fighting against error, but never out of an agitated, defensive mind-set. As Raissa puts it:

> Error is like the foam on the waves, it eludes our grasp and keeps reappearing. The soul must not

exhaust itself fighting against the foam. Its zeal must be purified and calmed and, by union with the divine Will, it must gather strength from the depths.... And everything that can be saved will be saved. For our God has chosen to reign in humility, and it really seems as if he wishes to show himself only just as much as is necessary in order that the visible Church shall endure to the end and the gates of hell shall not prevail against it.[9]

Like all mystics, Raissa dwelt a great deal on the meaning of suffering. She thought that it was necessary, in the words of St. Paul, to "fill up those things which are wanting in the sufferings of Christ" (Colossians 1:24):"There is also a fulfillment of the Passion which can be given only by fallible creatures, and that is the struggle against the Fall, against the attraction of this world... against the attraction of so many sins which represent human happiness. That gift Jesus could not make to the Father; only *we* can make it. There is a mode of redeeming the world, and of suffering, which is available only to sinners."[10]

After Raissa's death in 1960, Jacques decided to publish selections from various notebooks and letters spanning the years 1906-1960, under the title of *Raissa's Journal*. The mystical prayer of Raissa, taking place in the midst of the hub of the Catholic intellectual and artistic world, indicates how necessary it is that all fruitful works have as their source the intimate knowledge of God.

SELF-EFFACEMENT

*Throughout the writings of Raissa, the impression is given
that she considered self-glorification to be the attitude most
contrary to holiness. We must be self-effacing not because of
false modesty, but out of a love for Christ. That love makes
us long to let him live in us and through us.*

My God I'm here before thee
I crumble into nothing before thee
I adore thy greatness
My need is immense
Have pity on me
Let thy spirit dwell in me
Let the Holy Spirit live in me
The love of the Father and the Son
So that I may love thee and thou me.[11]

Don't be afraid to help me by giving me the grace of
renouncement and the other virtues, for I see my
impotence so clearly that never again will I attribute
to myself the least of the good you will have worked
in me.[12]

O my God who created me, have pity on me, have
pity on your poor little creature.... My Jesus and my
God! My one and only Jesus! My one and only Beloved! Spirit of Love and Mercy. My beloved and
blessed Saviour! Blessed and beloved Mother. O my
Lord and my God, have pity on your little creature,
infinitely wretched.[13]

O my dear beloved, O my unique beloved—dearly bought, all the more loved. I say dearly because I am at the moment paying, but when I shall be fully in possession of my treasure [like the mother whose labor in childbirth is over] I shall find that I have given nothing—that all I have given is nothing in comparison with what I shall have received....[14]

Living in the world,
deprived of the help that
monks and nuns find in their
rule and their vows—deprived
as well through a very special dispensation
of Providence, of the poverty
in which we lived for years—
and which God loves—we must make up
by inner fervour
and by poverty of spirit
for what we lack in outer supports.
So let us set ourselves diligently to practise
a deep and universal humility,
to make constant acts of thanksgiving
for so many blessings received,
to live in utter trust,
wholly abandoned to God's mercy.
Let us be kindly to all creatures.
Let us refrain from judging
the innermost of souls,
and let us open our heart wide enough
to admire everywhere,
and understand as much as possible

the liberty, the breadth and variety
of God's ways.[15]

God, my God, have pity on me, allow me to live in
your presence, with an upright soul, wholly lifted
toward You; a sincere soul, drinking in your sweet
Veracity; a very humble soul, looking only to you for
all its good. But a soul that has also great confidence
in its Father's goodness, and receives the manifesta-
tions of Your Love as simply as a child....

How could I stop being intent on knowing
whether I have advanced even one step toward you
or gone backwards?... You cannot be offended by
the attentiveness with which the soul scrutinizes and
conjectures your dispositions toward it.... You cannot reproach it for hoping in your mercy and believing in your love for us. Certainly we can gravely de-
ceive ourselves. But you will not impute this to our
pride, you know that it may be the consequence of
our human weakness and of the very obscurity of
Faith.

It seems to me that you ought rather to be touched
by the fervour of our thanksgiving when, even
though we are not sure, *we* think we have perceived
an effect of your love in us.

Is not our confidence more meritorious for being
able to spring up in uncertainty? We long so much
for your love that the faintest sign of its presence
gives us more joy than the most definite joys we
receive from creatures.[16]

O Hidden God, Your presence overwhelms my
    heart....
Now must I vigil keep before the gates of self,
Of my own self, a closely-shuttered tower
Whose secret walls my Lord Himself has shaped....
Our God of Compassion who restores what we have
    ruined—
I know not what He does,
Nor what He gives to me, what He obtains,
How He transforms my sin, to fashion light.
This aspect of myself which God creates in me
Only He knows, because He wills it thus....
Let us keep watch by everlasting gates
The long night through
Until the dawn when God shall tell the soul
To enter into self, and into Him.[17]

THE PASSION OF OUR LORD
AND HUMAN SUFFERING

*Raissa's response to her own sufferings and to those
around her was always to unite pain to the passion of
Christ and to make heroic interior acts of confidence in
God's providence. Typical of her insight is this first passage
about World War II.*

You cannot imagine... how deeply the events of the
last six years have filled my soul with dust and ashes;
events to which it is not possible to reconcile oneself
in any shape or manner except by naked, arid faith
in the divine Wisdom and Mercy, which not only

surpass our feelings, which I thought I knew—but, as I know now, surpass them in going beyond any standard of measurement, even thought of as supernatural. Human madness and human cruelty have been given permission to go to all lengths, unchecked, and, speaking of the six million massacred of whom so little is said, we counted very close friends among them.... And when one can put a name to a few of those who died in Auschwitz, in Belsen or in Dachau, and call up a face among them, the vast sorrow one feels for all the other victims itself assumes a face which haunts you with unspeakable horror and compassion. In spite of all this, God preserves in our souls a weight and stability of peace which I cannot understand; it is thus, no doubt, and much more powerfully still, that he preserved the souls of martyrs against despair.[18]

O Jesus, how necessary your Passion was. How necessary it was that your adorable heart should be pierced for me. O Jesus! O Jesus! your sorrowful and bleeding heart tells me not to be afraid and to have confidence.... You know, O Creator of all things, what a living heart is, a heart of flesh and blood where earth and heaven battle. You know that the human heart which seeks you has to suffer, to die a thousand deaths, in order to find you....

I abandon my heart to you, ready to suffer it to be wholly consumed in a faithful holocaust until the fire of divine charity, inextinguishable, soars above the cinders of all my earthly forces.[19]

Heavenly and blessed Father
See me here before you
With Veronica's veil on my face
The veil that bears the Holy Face.

At the sight of the features of Jesus
May your mercy be aroused
And may it deliver me from evil.

O you who created me, have pity on me.[20]

"The dew of the Lord is a dew of light." (Isaiah 26:19)
... Dispossessed, I chew the cud of anguish,
Parched with thirst for Your compassion,
For Your redemption
Of those who were taken away in chains
Up to the threshold of despair
And there were done to death.
When You join once again those scattered bones
Will they be clothed in flesh for another life?
When shall we hear the singing which brings to-
     gether opposites?

The joy-awakening melody
Will nevermore awake in me.
A sigh is all my breath
And my prayer a cry from the depth.
My spirit is absent, roving,
Lost in You,
Divided from me by fiery dew.[21]

LOVE OF NEIGHBOR

For Raissa love of neighbor certainly meant concern for the felt needs of others, but also for their unspoken spiritual needs. She resolves "not to see in my neighbour anything but the love with which God loves him, and his wretchedness as a creature which is no greater than my own wretchedness and which makes God himself pity us and draws down his mercy on us. All the rest is vanity and pettiness." [22]

In a charming short passage, she explains: "I love the saints because they are lovable; and the sinners because they are like me." [23] *Neighbor also included, for Raissa, Mary and the saints who love us and care for our needs.*

Lord... give me a new heart... triumphing, through the effusion of your Love, over itself, and over the sins of others, drawing them to you by firing them with your Love that is stronger than death.... It is a great torment, it is something almost inconceivable to one who loves you, the existence of all those people who do not know you, Truth so shining clear! Jesus, how is it possible! The soul cannot hold at the same time the deep knowledge of your Love and the thought of this world which is ignorant of you and seems to live without you. O Jesus, it would be easy for you to enlighten us all. Have pity on us. [24]

My God, I beseech You for our relatives and our benefactors; for our friends and our enemies; for the poor and the afflicted, for saints and sinners, for the sick and the dying, for the whole Church and for all souls; and especially for those, among the living and the dead, who have a particular need of prayers.[25]

If I have other joys, those that come from the affection and the blessed presence of Jacques—and of Vera and of Mother—I know very well that if one day you definitely made it known to me that your love had never dwelt in my soul, all joy would be extinguished for me and I should have lost my reason for living.[26]

If I were sure of pleasing
Jesus, my Sweet Saviour
On earth, I should have already
A paradise in my heart.

And if Mary protects me
Her blessed Son will receive me
In the company of the Saints
Who walk with Him in his Paradise.

Like a wandering sheep
Whose shepherd is seeking it
Seek me, merciful Mother,
Bring me safe to my Lord....

St. Veronica, you whom the Lord
So richly repaid for your kindness

By leaving you, the dearest of Relics,
The print of His face on your napkin,

Ask one thing for us incessantly.
Ask for a love so generous
That in our souls will at last appear
The true image and likeness of God.[27]

19

Adrienne von Speyr
(1902–1967)

I went on the most venturesome expeditions in Grandmother's park and my mind was entirely engaged in play. Yet I did not feel alienated. For instance, I could imagine that I was hiding together with my God. If, however, I had bothered another child while playing, I would have immediately forfeited the feeling of being able to pray, and that is how I recognized that it was wrong. I always had this standard of measure in the background: I noticed that I was alienated from myself when I could not find God just as easily in an activity as I found him, for instance, when starting to pray.[1]

✠ ✠ ✠

As WE MOVE IN HISTORY from the Middle Ages to our own times, we move also from intriguing, delightful, somewhat exotic figures of the past, to women whose stories and spiritual styles are more identifiable with our own. In contemporary terminology, Adrienne would be a "career/mom" mystic!

She was certainly a busy woman: doctor, married,

taking care of the children of her husband's first marriage, widowed, converted from Protestantism to the Catholic faith, then remarried. Led into deep mystical prayer, Adrienne found time to share the fruits of her contemplation in a startling array of works, including a meditative exegesis of the Gospel of St. John.[2]

Who was Adrienne von Speyr? She was born in 1902 into a Swiss Protestant family of doctors and clergymen. Her entire life was to be marked by the total rejection she suffered as a child from her mother. This wound in fact led directly to her greatest gift. In her loneliness Adrienne allowed God's grace to draw her into a mystical perception of supernatural realities, especially an angel of God who taught her the beauty of solitude and stillness.

Through this contemplative attitude, Adrienne became quite joyful. Yet she was always concerned about the sufferings of others, including patients she would visit with her physician relatives. One uncle, a psychiatrist, would take Adrienne along on his visits to an institution for the mentally ill. He was amazed to see how the patients would take heart when Adrienne came along and how good her intuitions were about what might help them. Later on, she organized anonymous financial assistance for those she knew to be needy.

Adrienne dreamed of following along in the medical profession that had been so much a part of her family. When disabling tuberculosis interrupted her schooling, she was hardly expected to live. Adrienne was afflicted with severe health problems throughout her life, and also had to buck the opposition of her mother to the idea of *women* doctors.

Nonetheless, this dedicated woman persevered in her studies and eventually became a physician of great skill and empathy. Even though she saw from sixty to eighty patients a day, she was somehow still able to relate to each one personally. As a doctor, Adrienne prevented hundreds of abortions, brought healing to many marriages, and treated the poor for free.

Never a biological mother herself, Adrienne became the wife of a widowed professor of history and the stepmother of his children. After he died, she married again, another historian, Werner Kaegi.

One of the most fascinating aspects of the story of Adrienne von Speyr was the way the Holy Spirit introduced this Protestant woman to the realities known to Catholics by means of mystical prayer. How many Protestants have intimate conversations with St. Ignatius of Loyola?

By 1940, Adrienne was coming into the friendship that was to shape the rest of her life. Her spiritual relationship with Fr. Hans Urs von Balthasar, the famous Swiss theologian, was to bring her into the Catholic church. Eventually he would become a member of her household. When she became too disabled to write the locutions that would come in a steady stream in her mystical prayer, he would sit by her bedside and take dictation. Together they would found the Secular Institute of Our Lady of the Way.

The writings of Adrienne von Speyr are unlike anything I have ever read. Perhaps the unusual style flowed from her long years of careful medical observation without admixture of personal subjective response. Everything we read in the books of Adrienne von Speyr seems to record something directly seen. Yet they are unlike the very sensate descriptions of the daily lives of Jesus and Mary that can be found in the works of mystics like Blessed Mary of Agreda. In the case of Adrienne's sharings, she depicts the *essence* of a reality. Here is an example from *The Handmaid of the Lord* concerning Mary's consent to the message of the angel Gabriel:

> Her fruitfulness is so unlimited only because the renunciation in her assent is also boundless. She sets no conditions, she makes no reservations; she gives herself completely in her answer. Before God she forgets all caution because the boundlessness of the divine plan opens before her eyes. ... In saying Yes, she has no wish, no preference, no demands which must be taken into consideration. She enters into no contract with God; she wishes only to be accepted in grace, as in grace she had been claimed by God.[3]

Without referring to herself or to the reader, Adrienne seems to be inviting us to share in Mary's experience, to let go of our own secret demands on life, that we might become more fruitful in the life of grace.

The spirituality of Adrienne von Speyr is essentially scriptural. As von Balthasar writes in his bio-graphical sketch *First Glance at Adrienne von Speyr:*

> Into confused and perplexing situations, she brings directions and solutions of penetrating, often painful clarity. But they are directions which all flow from the source-waters of biblical revelation.
>
> God is truth, and he makes a gift of his truth to man, who is then in the truth only if he lives in God's truth. That means for today: not in intro-spection, not by individual and social psychology does man come to the truth. If applied psychol-ogy is authentic, it will help man to get away from himself and become free for God and neighbor. Authentic existential analysis will disclose to man his decadence, his lovelessness, his need for re-deeming grace and for following the way he has been shone.
>
> Man is in the truth if, being open himself, he lives in the truth of God... above all the truth of the divine love... the divine Trinity.... With that, every artificially created barrier between heaven and earth, this life and the life to come, col-lapses....[4]

In other words, the path to peace and fullness lies not in the self-torture of constant analysis, but rather in the surrendering openness of Christian con-templation.

Adrienne died in 1967 after many years of intense suffering from heart disease, diabetes, arthritis, and blindness. She had already been well-known in Europe. Her spiritual writings are now becoming just as fruitful in the United States.

The last of these prayers I have included speak about deepening our daily life as part of our church. The contemplative life is a continual movement from the Eucharist, as the center of the real presence, to the smaller experiences of the presence of God deep within our own hearts in our interior prayer. This mystic teaches us never to choose one without the other.

We are called not to the church without any contemplative opening to God's love nor to mysticism severed from church life. Rather we are called to embrace the one way, truth, and life which is Christ —the bridegroom of his church as mystical body and his church in our own hearts.

OBEDIENCE

The necessity for obedience is not a popular topic in these times of individualism and rebellion. The following prayers will give us a greater sense of how profound this virtue really is.

Father in heaven, you divided the day from the night so that both might become a reminder and a joy for us: a reminder for us to think of you; a joy in serving you in every way. And so this day which is now breaking should also belong to you. It should become a day of your Church, a day of your children. It is still quite fresh, and it is as though anything could still be formed out of it. And we know that it is your possession, for you have created it, and that in obedience to you we should make of it a chosen day, a space in which you can be at home at every moment and everywhere, a space which is filled by you, but in which you also demand of us that we serve the mission which you point out to us. Help us to be pure, give us a good disposition, help us to do joyfully what our service requires.[5]

Dear Lord, you see how we become used to everything. Once, we gladly took up your service with the firm intent of being wholly surrendered to you. But, since every day brings nearly the same thing over and over again, it seems to us that our prayer has been circumscribed. We limit it to ourselves and to what seems necessary for just the task at hand so that in the end our spirit has assumed the size of this small task. We ask you not to allow us to narrow ourselves in this way; expand us again; bestow on us again some of the power of Mary's consent, which awaits in readiness the entire divine will, which is always as all-embracing as when it was first pronounced and which is daily conformed anew. She may have been glad or afraid or hopeful, weary of the daily work or led to the cross: always she stood before you as at first, obeying everything you said, hoping to do everything you wished. Behind every one of your wishes, even the smallest, she saw the great unlimited will of the Father which you, the Son, were fulfilling.[6]

Lord, you know that I want to serve you but am always still hanging on to my work and opinion; that again and again I hastily crawl back into myself in order to consider everything from my point of view: that I do this, in order to avoid that, wish this and abhor that. But, in your whole life on earth and especially on the cross, you have shown us what it means to do the will of another. For you, this other person was the Father, a Father so perfect that, from the beginning and without forming your own opinion, you considered and accepted each of his decisions as perfect. You did this not through an insight which would have been the result each time of examination and deliberation, but out of love. Your love for the Father has once and for all taken the place of every personal examination. And this love you also bestowed on your saints.... Give us your filial strength; grant that we learn to love the Father as you love him. Grant that we reach him through you and your attitude, that we become obedient by your perfect obedience....[7]

Her prayer as an infirm and elderly woman: I can no longer walk, can no longer work, can no longer choose for myself what I can sacrifice to you during the day. Sacrifice has taken on a different form now: I must simply accept everything and can only offer you always anew the desire that everything may take place according to your will.... I ask you to help me also in my weariness so that I may not tire of sacrificing everything to you. And bless this suffering for your whole Church and for all who seek the way to you. Amen.[8]

Lord of omnipotence and Lord of impotence, you reveal everything simultaneously in your holiness: your omnipotence which has the power to conquer and lead each one of us and your impotence which is dependent on the love and surrender of each one of us. You place all your holiness, as the light in which he can walk, at the disposal of each one who is ready to walk the way which you yourself are and which you prepare for him.[9]

DETACHMENT

Obedience and detachment are reciprocal. In an attitude of obedience we cannot be clinging desperately to our own plan for our lives, our own insistence on what is indispensable to our happiness.

Lord, deliver me and take me to yourself. You have shown me the fetters that hold me back on my way, and if they are still a hindrance, it is most likely because my innermost being I am not yet willing to separate myself from them. How often do I sigh and regret having so little freedom, yet I am only thinking of the bonds which come with my daily life and profession. But these bonds do not really obstruct the path, they do not influence its actual course, or at most only its exterior form; perhaps on the whole they are only minor trials. What weighs heavily does not come from outside; it lives and is formed in my own self; it is all that I am attached to, all that I do not want to do without, that serves as support and consolation, all that I believe myself entitled to. Take, Lord—I am trying to ask this earnestly of you— everything that in my eyes belongs to the legitimate possession of my soul but which paralyzes my love for you, which makes your love for my neighbor come to a standstill and freeze within me. Grant that I may disappear in the flow of your love to all men, so that it may pour forth unimpeded. Amen.[10]

Prayer at the beginning of Mass: ... Bless this hour... that we may stand before you detached from ourselves so as to see only you. That we will at last follow the path away from ourselves, toward you. That during this hour we will not think of everything possible that has nothing to do with you, but rather that we will pray for that to which you direct us, with an open spirit, because you open your Spirit to us; with a humble heart, because you want to dwell in such hearts; with a loving soul, because you are love itself. Bless us, open us, bestow on us your love. Amen.[11]

A prayer based on the famous one of St. Ignatius of Loyola: Take, Lord, and receive. Take my whole life; take it, I ask you, just as it is now, with all that it is, with my strengths, my intentions and efforts, but also with everything that still pulls away from you, that I have set aside for myself; take all of that, too, together with the rest that I offer you. Take everything that all may be yours....

All my liberty. The liberty of my days, the liberty of my thoughts, the liberty of my work, even the liberty of my prayer. From all this liberty, fashion a pure service of your own liberty, dispose freely of mine, therefore, see in it nothing except my desire to serve you. That is the choice that I now make as I leave all my liberty to you.

My memory, my understanding, and my entire will. Take my memory that it may no longer be filled with things that belong to me, but may be emptied and at your disposal in a new way, in order to receive only what you put into it.... And take my understanding which clung to so much, sought to comprehend so much that was not of you....

All that I have and possess, thou hast given all to me. You have given me the things that I need for living, my daily food, life with all its small, often superfluous comforts. You have also given me time from your own store of time, days for working, nights for resting.... All this is your gift and I have no right to anything....

Give me thy love and thy grace. Your love was always the triune, divine love in which you gave us a share and which we forfeited through our sins. This time give it to me in such a way that I will esteem it as the highest good.... I need it more urgently than the air I breathe; let me need it so urgently that it becomes a stimulus to serve you better....

For I am rich enough. Rich and capable of serving you, for in your love is contained everything needed by one who believes and hopes.[12]

Only the Lord can plant, to us perhaps he leaves the gathering of a few ears of his corn that have sprouted; we offer him what was already his. A living fire does not stop burning until everything has been consumed and turned to ashes; no one, however, pays attention to the ashes. Scattered on the earth, lifeless, hidden as they are, they cannot fertilize, but they can still be ground completely into the earth, serving a function of which they know nothing. Lord, burn us to ashes and scatter us according to your will. Should I ever still say what I want, do not grant it; even against all appearances, believe that I am yours alone and know no other will but yours. Amen.[13]

SACRAMENTAL AND LITURGICAL PRAYER

Some mystical writers take the life of the sacraments and of liturgy for granted, preferring to write about what pertains only to private prayer. Adrienne—like quite a number of the other women mystics represented in this book—is not only nourished by the shared realities of all Catholics but also contributes to others her contemplative insights into them.

Concerning listening to the sermon at Mass: Grant to us who listen a keen mind so that we really perceive your word and so not, in our faultfinding, merely become annoyed by the mediocrity of what is said, by the imperfect manner of expression, eventually seeing only the preacher and his weakness and nothing more of your word and Spirit. Rather, let this hour become a sacred hour where the mediator and the listener are united in your Spirit. Grant that we accept your word as the living word of God and allow it to become effective in us, that we take it home with us afterwards, so that a bit of the Church may come into being where we are....[14]

Before the tabernacle: Lord, I want to thank you for your presence, for recognizing in this house the house of your Father, and for dwelling within it, so as not to be distant and hidden from us with the Father and the Spirit, but rather to remain among us as the way that leads to the Father, as the way by which we will also attain the possession of the Holy Spirit. I want to thank you for being here, veiled in the mystery of the host, but so fully present that you yourself teach us to pray and help us to live. You are so fully present that we come to receive from you and take with us what your presence bestows upon us: the certainty of faith, the love of your dwelling among us. Lord, you know how weak and distracted we are and how we consider everything else more important than you; but again and again you guide us back to this place where you dwell in order to change us.[15]

After Confession: Lord,... while we have so often not lived up to your expectation, today, through grace, we can have the debris removed from us. You purify, you clear away, in us and together with us you accomplish something new. And all of this through the power of your cross.... And the absolution which you give us is a perfect one... you give back to us a new purity. And thus we need not continue to build on what was imperfect and weak, but may begin anew on the foundation of your own perfection, which you impart.[16]

The following prayers focus on the Creed:
"On the third day he rose again from the dead."... Allow us, Lord, to be drawn up with him, to dare the attempt to arise from our graves with you, even if this increases the weight of what you have to drag along. Let none of us perish and decay; take us all with you to God.[17]

"I believe in the Holy Spirit."... In allowing him to send us the Spirit from above, you prove to us that you received your Son, who returned to you with his mission fulfilled, in such a way that henceforth the graces will not cease to descend from heaven to earth. And thus in the Spirit you have made us the gift of never-ending hope. Father, let it be ours.[18]

"One holy Catholic Church." Lord, you have left us your holy Catholic Church as your bride who would tell us about you, her bridegroom, and make him come alive in us. Before the Father and the Holy Spirit, in the community of your Mother and all the saints, you profess to be the bridegroom of this

Church. With all of them you are at our disposal in the Church which you founded as an indissoluble union of love for the salvation of the world which was on the verge of being lost. Thus we thank you, Lord, for the gift of your Church.[19]

"Forgiveness of sins." ... And you show us the way to extricate ourselves from our sins: we should look more toward you than toward our sins, should trust more in your grace than we fear from our sins. For your forgiveness is more than merely a wiping away of our guilt; it is fulfilled in seeing you, in the love which you give us to pass on to our brothers. Where there was sin, there is now no gaping void; rather, your face is shining there: let us transmit this radiance to everyone around us.[20]

Notes

ONE
Saint Hildegard of Bingen

1. *Symphonia* trans. by Barbara Newman (Ithaca: Cornell University Press, 1988), 159-161.
2. Information for the biographical section of this chapter is taken from *Scivias* by Hildegard of Bingen, trans. by Mother Columba Hart and Jane Bishop with an intro. by Barbara Newman (New York: Paulist Press, 1990).
3. See *Scivias*, 278.
4. Ibid., 59.
5. Ibid., 67.
6. See Barbara Newman's intro. to *Scivias*, 17.
7. *Scivias*, 18-19.
8. *Symphonia*, 99.
9. Ibid., 263.
10. Ibid., 143-147.
11. Ibid., 155.
12. Ibid., 113.
13. Ibid., 130-131.
14. Ibid., 135.
15. Ibid., 251.
16. Ibid., 253.
17. Ibid., 255.

TWO
Blessed Angela of Foligno

1. *The Book of Divine Consolation*, trans. by Mary G. Steegman with an intro. by Algar Thorold (New York: Cooper Square Publishers, Inc., 1966), 224-225.
2. Ibid., 4-5.
3. Ibid., 12.

4. Ibid., 15.
5. Ibid., 14.
6. Ibid., xxv.
7. Ibid.
8. Ibid., 184-185.
9. Ibid., 159-161.
10. Ibid., 162.
11. Ibid., 166
12. Ibid., 170.
13. Ibid., 185.
14. Ibid., 208-209.
15. Ibid., 219.
16. Ibid., 170.
17. Ibid., 198-199.
18. Ibid., 207-208.
19. Ibid., 214-216.
20. Ibid., 202.
21. Ibid., 211-212.
22. Ibid., 219-220.

THREE
Saint Gertrude the Great

1. *The Exercises of Saint Gertrude*, intro., commentary and trans. by a Benedictine nun of Regina Laudis who wished to remain anonymous (Westminster: The Newman Press, 1956), 116.
2. Ibid., xii.
3. Contained in *The Life and Revelations of Saint Gertrude* (Westminster: The Newman Press, 1949).
4. *Exercises*, see above.
5. Ibid., 7.
6. Ibid., 85.
7. *The Life and Revelations of Saint Gertrude*, 76-77.
8. *Gertrude the Great of Helfta: Spiritual Exercises*, trans. and intro. by Gertrude J. Lewis and Jack Lewis (Kalamazoo: Cistercian Publications, 1989), 38.
9. *The Exercises of Saint Gertrude*, 85.
10. Ibid., 88.
11. Ibid., 172.
12. Ibid., 91.
13. Ibid., 162.

14. Ibid., 170.
15. Ibid., 119-130.

FOUR
Hadewijch of Belgium

1. *Hadewijch: The Complete Works,* trans. and intro. by Mother Columba Hart, O.S.B. (Mahwah: Paulist Press, 1980), 352. Biographical information for this chapter is taken from this book.
2. Ibid., 174.
3. Ibid., 344-345.
4. Ibid., 178.
5. Ibid., 50.
6. Ibid., 246.
7. Ibid., 256.
8. Ibid., 248.
9. Ibid., 191.
10. Ibid., 174.
11. Ibid., 185.

FIVE
Saint Birgitta of Sweden

1. *Revelations of St. Birgitta of Sweden* by Anthony Butkovich (Los Angeles: Ecumenical Foundation of America, 1972), 50. Biographical information about St. Birgitta comes from this book and *St. Bridget of Sweden* by Johannes Jorgensen, Vols. I and II, trans. by Ingeborg Lund (London: Longmans Green and Co., 1954).
2. Jorgensen, 21.
3. Butkovich, xv.
4. Ibid., 3.
5. Jorgensen, 185-186.
6. Ibid., 7.
7. Ibid., 10.
8. Ibid., 99-100.
9. Ibid., 35-38.
10. Ibid., 3.
11. Ibid., 47-48.
12. Ibid., 48.
13. Ibid., 49.
14. Ibid., 50.

SIX
Blessed Julian of Norwich

1. Julian of Norwich, *Revelations of Divine Love,* trans. with an intro. by M.L. del Mastro (Garden City: Image, Doubleday, 1977), 143. Biographical information for this chapter comes from this book.
2. Ibid., 83-84.
3. Ibid., 88.
4. Ibid., 191.
5. Ibid., 195.
6. Ibid., 97.
7. Ibid., 88-89.
8. Ibid., 91.
9. Ibid., 93.
10. Ibid., 101-102.
11. Ibid., 124-125.
12. Ibid., 104-105.
13. Ibid., 130.
14. Ibid., 106.

SEVEN
Saint Catherine of Siena

1. *The Dialogue* by St. Catherine, trans. by Suzanne Noffke, O.P. (Mahwah: Paulist Press, 1980), 49-50.
2. Biographical information about St. Catherine comes mostly from Raymond of Capua, *The Life of Catherine of Siena,* trans. by Conleth Kearns, O.P. (Wilmington: Michael Glazier, 1980).
3. *Dialogue,* 54.
4. Ibid., 8.
5. Ibid., 9.
6. Raymond of Capua, 83.
7. *Dialogue,* 125.
8. Ibid., 279.
9. Ibid., 71-72.
10. Ibid., 264.
11. Ibid., 189-190.
12. Ibid., 49-50.
13. Ibid., 230-231.
14. Ibid., 238-239.

15. Ibid., 275.
16. Ibid., 63.
17. Ibid., 273.
18. Ibid., 325-326.
19. Ibid., 365-366.

EIGHT
Saint Joan of Arc

Biographical information for this chapter is drawn from the following books, as well as *Butler's Lives of the Saints*, Vol. II, edited, revised, and supplemented by Herbert J. Thurston, S.J., and Donald Attwater (Westminster: Christian Classics, 1956), 427-431.

1. Mary Neill, O.P. and Ronda Chervin, *Great Saints, Great Friends* (Staten Island: Alba House, 1990), 64.
2. Mark Twain, *Joan of Arc* (San Francisco: Ignatius Press, 1989), 14.
3. Wilfred T. Jewkes and Jerome B. Landfield, *Joan of Arc: Fact, Legend and Literature* (New York: Harcourt, Brace and World, Inc., 1964), 10.
4. Hilaire Belloc, *Joan of Arc* (New York: The Declan X. McMullen Co., Inc., 1949), 7-8.
5. Jewkes and Landfield, 7.
6. Neill and Chervin, 56-57.
7. Jewkes and Landfield, 8.
8. Ibid., 9.
9. Ibid., 12.
10. Ibid., 12-14.
11. Ibid., 15.
12. Ibid., 16-17.
13. Ibid., 18.
14. Ibid., 19.
15. Ibid., 32.
16. Ibid., 40.
17. Ibid., 79.
18. Ibid., 78.
19. Ibid., 79.

NINE
Saint Catherine of Genoa

1. *The Life and Sayings of St. Catherine of Genoa*, trans. and edited by Paul Garvin (Staten Island: Alba House, 1964),

32. The information for this introduction is taken primarily from this book.

2. Ibid., 23.
3. Ibid., 24-25.
4. Ibid., 27.
5. Ibid., 41-42.
6. Ibid., 50.
7. Ibid., 54.
8. Ibid., 58.
9. Ibid., 81.
10. Ibid., 122-123.
11. Ibid., 65.
12. Ibid., 68.
13. Ibid., 69.
14. Ibid., 85.
15. Ibid.
16. Ibid., 98.
17. Ibid., 68.
18. Ibid., 89.
19. Ibid., 90.
20. Ibid., 107.
21. Ibid., 116.
22. Ibid.
23. Ibid., 66.
24. Ibid., 99.

TEN
Saint Teresa of Avila

1. Famous exhortation of St. Teresa used by herself as a bookmark.
2. Information on the life and writings of St. Teresa is taken primarily from *The Complete Works of St. Theresa*, edited by Allison Peers (London: Sheed and Ward, 1946).
3. For this quotation from the *Autobiography* and more of Teresa on spiritual friendship, see *Spiritual Friendship: The Darkness and the Light* by Ronda Chervin (Boston: St. Paul Books and Media, 1992).
4. *Complete Works.* Vol. II, 402-420.
5. Ibid., 402.
6. Ibid., 403-404.
7. Ibid., 405.

8. Ibid., 408-409.
9. Ibid., 403.
10. Ibid., 409.
11. Ibid., 411.
12. Ibid., 406-407.
13. Ibid., 414.
14. Ibid., 416.
15. Ibid., 419-420.
16. Ibid., 407.
17. Ibid., 414.
18. Ibid., 417.
19. Ibid., 418-419.

ELEVEN
Saint Rosa of Lima

1. Frances Parkinson Keyes, *The Rose and the Lily* (New York: Hawthorn Books, Inc., 1961), 108 and footnote 31, 233.
2. Information about the life of St. Rosa of Lima comes from the book by Keyes, *Rose of America* by Sara Maynard (London: Sheed and Ward, 1943), and Mary Fabyan Windeatt, *Angel of the Andes* (Paterson: St. Antony Guild Press).
3. Keyes, 93.
4. Ibid., 133.
5. Ibid.
6. Ibid., 135.
7. Ibid., 129-130.
8. Ibid., 142.
9. Ibid., 132.
10. Ibid., 234, footnote 42.
11. Ibid., 124.

TWELVE
Blessed Marie of the Incarnation

1. *Marie of the Incarnation Selected Writings*, edited by Irene Mahoney, O.S.U. (New York: Paulist Press, 1989), 109-110. Information for this chapter comes primarily from this book.
2. Ibid., 41.
3. Ibid., 49.
4. Ibid., 12.
5. Ibid., 16.
6. Ibid., 138-139.

7. Ibid., 197.
8. Ibid., 205.
9. Ibid., 149-150.
10. Ibid., 275-276.
11. Ibid., 194-219.
12. Ibid., 201-202.
13. Ibid., 202.
14. Ibid., 208.
15. Ibid., 218.
16. Ibid., 200.
17. Ibid., 211-212.
18. Ibid., 215.

THIRTEEN
Blessed Mary of Agreda

1. *Mystical City of God*, Vol. IV, by Sister Mary of Jesus (Blessed Mary of Agreda), trans. by Fiscar Marison (Albuquerque: Corcoran Publishing Co., 1902), 66.
2. The information in this biographical section is taken from the intro. to Vol. I of the four-volume *Mystical City of God* by Sister Mary of Jesus (Blessed Mary of Agreda).
3. See Frontispiece of Vol. I of the *Mystical City of God*.
4. *Mystical City of God*, Vol. I, 35-37.
5. Ibid., ix ff.
6. Ibid., xv-xvi.
7. Ibid., 162-163.
8. Ibid., 284-285.
9. Ibid., 532-535.
10. Ibid., 276-277.
11. Ibid., 311.
12. *Mystical City of God*, Vol. IV, 116-117.
13. Ibid., 108-109.
14. *Mystical City of God*, Vol. III, 39-41.
15. Ibid., 472-473.
16. Ibid., 643.

FOURTEEN
Saint Margaret Mary Alacoque

1. *These Three Hearts* by Margaret Yeo (Milwaukee: The Bruce Publishing Co., 1940), 188. Most of the information for this chapter comes from this book about Blessed Claude de la

Colombière, Saint Margaret Mary Alacoque, and the Sacred Heart, and from *Lives of the Saints,* edited by Joseph Vann, O.F.M. (New York: John J. Crawley and Co., Inc., 1954).

2. Yeo, 121.
3. Ibid., 144-145.
4. Ibid., 163.
5. Ibid., 187.
6. *Lives of the Saints,* 429.
7. Yeo, 180.
8. Ibid., 192-193.
9. Ibid., 128.
10. Ibid., 168.
11. Ibid., 236.
12. Ibid., 274.

FIFTEEN
Blessed Mariam Baouardy

1. Brunot, Amedée, S.C.J. *Mariam: The Little Arab,* trans. by Jeanne Dumais, O.C.D.S., and Sister Miriam of Jesus, O.C.D. (Eugene: The Carmel of Maria Regina, 1990), 36. The biographical information for this chapter comes from this book.
2. Ibid., i-iv.
3. Ibid., 25.
4. Ibid., 51, 56.
5. Ibid., 55, 60, 71.
6. Ibid., 21-22.
7. Ibid., 29.
8. Ibid., 41-42.
9. Ibid., 98.
10. Ibid., 54.
11. Ibid., 46.
12. Ibid., 47-48.
13. Ibid., 48.
14. Ibid., 47.
15. Ibid., 48-49.
16. Ibid., 52-53, 56.
17. Ibid., 22.
18. Ibid., 46.
19. Ibid., 116.

SIXTEEN
Concepción Cabrera de Armida (Conchita)

1. *Conchita: A Mother's Spiritual Diary*, edited by M.M. Philipon, O.P., trans. by Aloysius J. Owens, S.J. (Staten Island: Alba House, 1978), 29. Most of the information used in this chapter come from this book.
2. Ibid., 27.
3. Ibid., 20.
4. Ibid., 38.
5. Ibid., 49-51.
6. *Before the Altar*, trans. by Luisa Icaza de Medina Mora, intro. by Most Reverend Donald W. Montrose (Mexico: Ediciones Cimiento, A.C., 1913, 1988).
7. Ibid., 7.
8. Ibid., 12-14.
9. Ibid., 14-16.
10. Ibid., 24.
11. Ibid., 8-10.
12. Ibid., 24-25.
13. Ibid., 27-28.
14. Ibid., 10-12.
15. Ibid., 127-128.
16. Ibid., 56.
17. Ibid., 25-26.
18. Ibid., 35-37.
19. Ibid., 83.

SEVENTEEN
Blessed Elizabeth of the Trinity

1. *Light, Love, Life: Elizabeth of the Trinity—A Look at the Face and Heart*, text and illustrations edited by Conrad De Meester, O.C.D., trans. by Sister Aletheia Kane, O.C.D. (Washington, D.C.: I.C.S. Publications, 1987), 112.
2. Information for this chapter comes primarily from the above book, from *The Spiritual Doctrine of Blessed Elizabeth of the Trinity* by Luigi Borriello, O.C.D, trans. by Jordan Aumann, O.P. (Staten Island: Alba House, 1986) and from *Elizabeth of the Trinity: The Complete Works*, Vol. I, trans. by Sister Aletheia Kane, O.C.D. (Washington, D.C.: I.C.S. Publications: 1984.)

3. *The Complete Works,* Vol. I, 142.
4. Ibid., 179.
5. Ibid., 162.
6. Ibid., 32.
7. Ibid., 24-25.
8. Ibid., 26.
9. Ibid., 183.
10. Ibid., 14.
11. Ibid., 16.
12. Ibid., 17.
13. Ibid., 94-95.

EIGHTEEN
Raissa Maritain

1. *Raissa's Journal* presented by Jacques Maritain (Albany: Magi Books, 1974), 316-317.
2. Information for this chapter comes from *We Have Been Friends Together* by Raissa Maritain, trans. by Julie Kernan (New York: Longmans, Green and Co., Inc., 1942), *Adventures in Grace* by Raissa Maritain, trans. by Julie Kernan (New York: Longmans, Green and Co., Inc.: 1945), and *Raissa's Journal.*
3. See *We Have Been Friends Together.*
4 .*Raissa's Journal,* 255.
5. Ibid., 108.
6. Ibid., 35-36.
7. Ibid., xv.
8. Ibid., 229-230.
9. Ibid., 158.
10. Ibid., 247.
11. Ibid., 19-20.
12. Ibid., 28.
13. Ibid., 42.
14. Ibid., 61.
15. Ibid., 154.
16. Ibid., 168-169.
17. Ibid., 317-318.
18. Ibid., 303-304.
19. Ibid., 52-53.
20. Ibid., 297-298.

21. Ibid., 297-298.
22. Ibid., 38.
23. Ibid., 66.
24. Ibid., 136.
25. Ibid., 155.
26. Ibid., 170.
27. Ibid., 20-21.

NINETEEN
Adrienne von Speyr

1. *First Glance at Adrienne von Speyr* by Hans Urs von Balthasar, trans. by Antje Lawry and Sr. Sergia Englund, O.C.D. (San Francisco: Ignatius Press, 1981), 128. Information for this chapter comes primarily from this book.
2. All of the writings of Adrienne von Speyr are gradually being published in English through the auspices of Ignatius Press. I especially want to call attention to her classic about Our Lady: *Handmaid of the Lord*, trans. by E. A. Nelson (San Francisco: Ignatius Press, 1985), and the most profound meditative analysis of the sacrament of penance I have ever read: *Confession*, trans. by Douglas W. Stott (San Francisco: Ignatius Press, 1985).
3. *Handmaid of the Lord*, 9.
4. *First Glance*, 245-246.
5. Ibid., 195.
6. Ibid., 204.
7. Ibid., 205-206.
8. Ibid., 213.
9. Ibid., 223.
10. Ibid., 220.
11. Ibid., 196-197.
12. Ibid., 214-216.
13. Ibid., 222.
14. Ibid., 198.
15. Ibid., 201-202.
16. Ibid., 207.
17. Ibid., 227-228.
18. Ibid., 229.
19. Ibid., 230.
20. Ibid., 232.

Bibliography

Angela of Foligno, Blessed, *The Book of Divine Consolation*, translated by Mary G. Steegman, introduction by Algar Thorold (New York, New York: Cooper Square Publishers, Inc., 1966).

Balthasar, Hans Urs von, *First Glance at Adrienne von Speyr*, translated by Antje Lawry and Sr. Sergia Englund, O.C.D. (San Francisco, California: Ignatius Press, 1981).

Belloc, Hilaire, *Joan of Arc* (New York, New York: The Declan X. McMullen Company, Inc., 1949).

Borriello, Luigi, O.C.D., *The Spiritual Doctrine of Blessed Elizabeth of the Trinity*, translated by Jordan Aumann, O.P. (Staten Island, New York: Alba House, 1986).

Brunot, Amedee, S.C.J., *Mariam: The Little Arab*, translated by Jeanne Dumais, O.C.D.S., and Sister Miriam of Jesus, O.C.D. (Eugene, Oregon: The Carmel of Maria Regina, 1990).

Butler's Lives of the Saints, Volumes I-IV, edited, revised, and supplemented by Herbert J. Thurston, S.J., and Donald Attwater (Westminster, Maryland: Christian Classics, 1956).

Cabrera de Armida, Concepción (Conchita), *Before the Altar*, translated by Luisa Icaza de Medina Mora, introduction by Most Reverend Donald W. Montrose (Mexico: Ediciones Cimiento, A.C., 1913, 1988).

Catherine of Siena, St., *The Dialogue,* translated by Suzanne Noffke, O.P. (Mahwah, New Jersey: Paulist Press, 1980).

Chervin, Ronda, *A Treasury of Women Saints* (Ann Arbor, Michigan: Servant Publications, 1991).

Conchita: A Mother's Spiritual Diary, edited by M.M. Philipon, O.P., translated by Aloysius J. Owens, S.J. (Staten Island, New York: Alba House, 1978).

Elizabeth of the Trinity: the Complete Works, Vol. I, translated by Sister Aletheia Kane, O.C.D. (Washington, D.C.: I.C.S. Publications, 1984).

Gertrude the Great of Helfta: Spiritual Exercises, translated and introduced by Gertrude J. Lewis and Jack Lewis (Kalamazoo, Michigan: Cistercian Publications, 1989).

Gertrude, Saint, *The Exercises of Saint Gertrude*, translated with an introduction and commentary by a Benedictine nun who wishes to remain anonymous of Regina Laudis (Westminster, Maryland: The Newman Press, 1956).

Gertrude, Saint, *The Life and Revelations of Saint Gertrude* (Westminster, Maryland: The Newman Press, 1949).

Habig, Marion A., O.F.M., *The Franciscan Book of Saints* (Chicago, Illinois: Franciscan Herald Press, 1979).

Hadewijch of Belgium, *Hadewijch: The Complete Works*, translated and introduced by Mother Columba Hart, O.S.B. (Mahwah, New Jersey: Paulist Press, 1980).

Hildegard of Bingen, St., *Scivias*, translated by Mother Columba Hart and Jane Bishop (New York, New York: Paulist Press, 1990).

Hildegard of Bingen, St., *Symphonia*, introduction, translation and commentary by Barbara Newman (Ithaca, New York: Cornell University Press, 1988).

Jewkes, Wilfred T., and Landfield, Jerome B., *Joan of Arc: Fact, Legend and Literature* (New York, New York: Harcourt, Brace and World, Inc., 1964).

Jorgensen, Johannes, *St. Bridget of Sweden*, Vols. I and II, translated by Ingeborg Lund (London, England: Longmans Green and Co., 1954).

Julian of Norwich, *Revelations of Divine Love*, translated with an introduction by M.L. del Mastro (Garden City, New York: Image, Doubleday, 1977).

Keyes, Frances Parkinson, *The Rose and the Lily* (New York, New York: Hawthorn Books, Inc., 1961).

The Life and Sayings of St. Catherine of Genoa, translated and edited by Paul Garvin (Staten Island, New York: Alba House, 1964).

Light, Love, Life: Elizabeth of the Trinity—A Look at the Face and Heart, text and illustrations edited by Conrad De Meester,

O.C.D., translated by Sister Aletheia Kane, O.C.D. (Washington, D.C.: I.C.S. Publications, 1987).

Lives of the Saints, edited by Joseph Vann, O.F.M. (New York, New York: John J. Crawley and Co., Inc., 1954).

Lord, Bob and Penny, *Saints and Other Powerful Women in the Church* (Westlake Village, California: Journeys of Faith, 1989).

Marie of the Incarnation: Selected Writings, edited by Irene Mahoney, O.S.U. (New York, New York: Paulist Press, 1989).

Maritain, Raissa, *Adventures in Grace,* translated by Julie Kernan (New York, New York: Longmans, Green and Co., Inc., 1945).

Maritain, Raissa, *We Have Been Friends Together,* translated by Julie Kernan (New York, New York: Longmans, Green and Co., Inc., 1942).

Mary of Jesus, Sister (Blessed Mary of Agreda), *Mystical City of God,* four volumes, translated by Fiscar Marison (Albuquerque, New Mexico: Corcoran Publishing Co., 1902).

Maynard, Sara, *Rose of America* (London, England: Sheed and Ward, 1943).

Neill, Mary, O.P., and Chervin, Ronda, *Great Saints, Great Friends* (Staten Island, New York: Alba House, 1990).

Raissa's Journal, presented by Jacques Maritain (Albany, New York: Magi Books, 1974).

Raymond of Capua, *The Life of Catherine of Siena,* translated by Conleth Kearns, O.P. (Wilmington, Delaware: Michael Glazier, 1980).

Revelations of St. Birgitta of Sweden, edited by Anthony Butkovich (Los Angeles, California: The Ecumenical Foundation of America, 1972).

Sheed, Frank J., *Saints Are Not Sad* (New York, New York: Sheed and Ward, 1949).

Teresa of Avila, St., *The Complete Works of St. Teresa,* edited by Allison Peers (London, England: Sheed and Ward, 1946).

Twain, Mark, *Joan of Arc* (San Francisco, California: Ignatius Press, 1989).

Yeo, Margaret, *These Three Hearts* (Milwaukee, Wisconsin: The Bruce Publishing Co., 1940).

Another Book to Deepen Your Spiritual Life

Treasury of Women Saints
Ronda De Sola Chervin

You will be fascinated and inspired by these stories of over two hundred women saints. From mothers like Elizabeth of Hungary and prophetic saints like Hildegard of Bingen to mystics like Julian of Norwich, this treasury chronicles Catholicism's most beloved women saints from the early church to modern times.

Ideal for use in daily devotions, each of the two hundred entries provides a biographical sketch of one or more saints, a life application for the reader, and a prayer or meditation for the day. *Treasury of Women Saints* is an ideal devotional companion to the life and spirituality of the saints for you and your loved ones. *$11.99*

Available at your Christian bookstore or from:
**Servant Publications • Dept. 209 • P.O. Box 7455
Ann Arbor, Michigan 48107**
Please include payment plus $1.25 per book
for postage and handling.
*Send for our FREE catalog of Christian
books, music, and cassettes.*